CONVERSATIONS WITH WILLIE

Other works by Robin Maugham

Novels
THE SERVANT
LINE ON GINGER
THE ROUGH AND THE SMOOTH
BEHIND THE MIRROR
THE MAN WITH TWO SHADOWS
NOVEMBER REEF
THE GREEN SHADE
THE SECOND WINDOW
THE LINK
THE WRONG PEOPLE
THE LAST ENCOUNTER
THE BARRIER
THE SIGN
KNOCK ON TEAK
LOVERS IN EXILE

Short Stories
THE BLACK TENT AND OTHER STORIES

Travel
COME TO DUST
NOMAD
APPROACH TO PALESTINE
NORTH AFRICAN NOTEBOOK
JOURNEY TO SIWA
THE SLAVES OF TIMBUKTU
THE JOYITA MYSTERY

Biography
SOMERSET AND ALL THE MAUGHAMS

Autobiography
ESCAPE FROM THE SHADOWS
SEARCH FOR NIRVANA

CONVERSATIONS WITH WILLIE

Recollections of W. Somerset Maugham

Robin Maugham

W. H. ALLEN · LONDON
A Howard & Wyndham Company

1978

Printed and bound in Great Britain by
The Garden City Press Limited,
Letchworth, Hertfordshire SG6 1JS
for the Publishers, W. H. Allen & Co. Ltd,
44 Hill Street, London W1X 8LB

ISBN 0 491 02303 0

Most of the people who read books in Great Britain
borrow them freely from public libraries and do not buy
copies. As a result many authors find survival difficult.
If you want literature to survive, please support Public
Lending Right by writing to your local Member of
Parliament.

For
Peter Burton

Without whose help—as
has often been said, but
this time with truth—
this book could not have
been written.

ACKNOWLEDGEMENTS

I would like to thank the following for their assistance with this book: Spencer Curtis Brown; the Estate of the late W. Somerset Maugham, for permission to use the quotation from *For Services Rendered;* Mrs Jeanne Francis, for her secretarial help; Gordon Anderson, who took charge of the files of photographs from which the illustrations used in this book were selected; Peter Burton, for his research and assistance throughout the preparation and writing of the book.

I should also like to acknowledge the usefulness of Raymond Toole Stott's excellent *A Bibliography of the Works of W. Somerset Maugham,* which proved invaluable when checking details of publication of Willie's books.

ILLUSTRATIONS
Between pages 96 and 97

A typical page from the author's diary of his conversations with his uncle.

Maugham as a schoolboy, and aged seventeen.

Maugham as a young man.

The two brothers, Frederic and William.

Syrie.

Liza—Willie's daughter.

Gerald Haxton.

Willie and Robin at Parker's Ferry (1945), and at the Villa Mauresque (1959).

The cottage at Parker's Ferry, North Carolina, and the writing room.

Cartoons by Ronald Searle and Bernard Partridge.

The Moorish sign against the evil eye at the entrance and front door of the Villa Mauresque.

The swimming pool at the villa.

Alan Searle, and in the garden with Maugham.

Willie and Robin at the Villa Mauresque (1965).

Maugham on his ninetieth birthday, and aged ninety-one.

The opening of The Maugham Library at The King's School, Canterbury, and the funeral service.

Part One

Willie—as I called my uncle, William Somerset Maugham, since the days when I was a schoolboy—was certainly the most famous author alive. And he was probably the saddest.

This little, frail old man, with a wizened, wrinkled face like a Chinese sage, would shuffle through the vast, deserted rooms of the Villa Mauresque—his luxurious house on Cap Ferrat in the South of France—like a lost ghost. He sought comfort in the past. He was bewildered by the present, and afraid of the future.

When I stayed with him in 1965 in this famous villa on the Riviera, I was the first guest for several months.

"You know," he said to me, with his pronounced stammer, "I shall be dead very soon. And I der-don't like the idea of it at all."

The lines of his face were twisted in misery.

"I'm a very old party," he said. "But that doesn't make it any easier for me."

At the age of ninety-one my uncle William Somerset Maugham still made a fortune—even though he hadn't written a word for ages. The royalties from his books and short stories still literally flowed in from all over the world. And so did the fan-letters: he got more than three hundred a week—most of them from teenagers. (All of them were answered, and all replies were signed.) But he could no longer read the letters himself, for

3

cataracts had formed on both his eyes. His favourite pastime—reading—was now denied him.

At this moment four of his plays were running in Germany. His play *The Circle* had been brilliantly revived in England by Evelyn Laye and Frank Lawton, and *The Constant Wife* had just been turned into a musical.

One of his most famous novels, *Of Human Bondage*, was soon to be made into a film—which might bring him as many millions of dollars as did *Rain, The Moon and Sixpence* and *The Razor's Edge*.

Unfortunately, the one reward all Willie's talent and success had not given him was happiness.

"What is the happiest memory of your life?" I asked him as he sat beside me on the sofa at the Villa Mauresque.

"I cer-can't think of a single moment," he stammered.

I glanced at Alan Searle, his sixty-year-old secretary and friend who had been Willie's most loyal and devoted companion for over twenty years. I looked round the drawing-room at the immensely valuable furniture and pictures and objects that Willie's success had enabled him to acquire. I remembered that the villa itself, and the wonderful garden I could see through the windows —a fabulous setting on the edge of the Mediterranean— were worth £600,000.

Willie had eleven servants, including his cook, Annette, who was the envy of all the other millionaires on the Riviera. He dined off silver plates, waited on by Marius his butler and Henri his footman. But it no longer meant anything to him.

*　　　*　　　*

A broad corridor ran all the way round the upper

4

storey of the patio. The following afternoon of my stay, I found Willie reclining on a sofa, peering through his spectacles at a Bible which had very large print. He looked horribly wizened and his face was grim. As I walked along the corridor in a beach dressing-gown on my way to the swimming-pool, he looked up angrily at the intrusion.

"Good afternoon," I said. He did not recognise me. His hands began to tremble. He glared at me.

"What's that? What's that you said?"

I spoke loudly and distinctly. "I said 'Good Afternoon'."

Willie now recognised me, and his hands stopped trembling, but he was still in a bad mood.

"Well, at least your remark is apt and to the point—for it *is* a good afternoon," he said. "And once again I've been reading the Bible you gave me ... And I've come across the quotation—'What shall it profit a man if he gain the whole world and lose his own soul?' "

Willie clasped and unclasped his hands.

"I must tell you, my dear Robin, that the text used to hang opposite my bed when I was a child ... Of course, it's all a lot of bunk. But the thought is quite interesting all the same."

Willie took up a cigarette and I lit it for him.

"Where are you off to now?" he demanded.

"I was thinking of going for a swim in the pool," I replied.

"Won't you take me round the garden first?" he asked.

He walked slowly, leaning on my arm, along a green glade between the eucalyptus and pine trees.

"You know, when I die," he said, "they'll take it all away from me—every tree, the whole house, and every

5

stick of furniture. I shan't even be able to take a single table with me."

For a while he was silent as we walked through a grove of orange trees.

"Jesus Christ could cope with all the miseries I have had to contend with in life," he announced. Then he stopped walking and peered across the top of the trees towards the blue sea beyond. Suddenly he smiled sardonically, and there was a flash of Willie as he had been in his prime.

"But then Jesus Christ had certain advantages I don't possess," he said.

As I helped Willie down the steps towards the house, he stopped and turned to me.

"You know, dying is a very dull, dreary affair," he said. Then he smiled. It was a smile full of compassion for all the foibles of the human race.

"And my advice to you is to have nothing whatever to do with it," he concluded.

That evening in the drawing-room after dinner, Willie was standing by the fireplace. He was wearing an old smoking-jacket and a silk scarf. He put down his empty coffee cup on a side-table, then flung himself down on to the sofa. He looked up at me.

"Oh, Robin, I'm so tired, so tired..." he muttered. Then he gave a gulp of sorrow and buried his head in his hands.

"I've been a fer-failure the whole way through my life," he said. "I've made mistake after mistake. I've made a hash of everything."

I sat down on the sofa beside him and tried to comfort him.

"You're the most famous writer alive. Surely that means something?" I asked.

6

"I wish I'd never written a single word," he answered. "It's brought me nothing but misery . . . Everyone who's got to know me well has ended up by hating me . . . My whole life has been a failure . . ."

He took my hand. For an instant he was calmer.

"And now it's too late to change," he said. "It's too late."

Willie looked up and his grip tightened on my hand. He was staring towards the door. His face was contorted with fear, and he was trembling violently.

"Who's that coming into the room?" he asked.

Willie's face was now ashen as he stared in horror ahead of him. Suddenly he began to shriek.

"Go away!" he cried. "I'm not ready . . . I'm not dead yet . . . I'm not dead yet, I tell you . . ."

His high-pitched terror-struck voice seemed to echo from wall to wall. I looked round, but the room was empty as before.

"There's no one there, Willie," I told him.

Willie began to gasp hysterically. Then the attack passed. His grip on my hand relaxed. He lay back on the sofa and tried to smile. He spoke very quietly.

"You know, I'm at death's door," he said. "But the trouble is that I'm afraid to knock."

*　　　*　　　*

The reader of this book may well wonder how it was that over a dozen years after Willie's death I could remember scenes and dialogue so accurately. Let me explain.

As a child I had always admired my uncle, and when I grew up I realised how many people shared my admiration for his work. A few weeks before the New Year of 1945 I went to stay with Willie in North

Carolina. I then began to take notes of what he said, what he did, what he wore, and what he ate.

Willie spent the last few years of his life at his villa in Cap Ferrat. Each time I stayed with him and with his wonderfully kind and patient companion, Alan Searle, my interest in my Uncle Willie increased. By then I had become a writer myself, and my first novel, *The Servant,* had been a success. I could now think of my uncle as a fellow writer. Moreover, he fascinated me as an individual. I began to observe him carefully and to record my impressions in folio-sized notebooks.

Willie died in 1965. Shortly afterwards, I went to live in Spain. The notebooks—together with many other documents—went into store.

When I returned to England, after nearly ten years abroad, I was foraging through the various papers which had been stored, and I came across—dusty and a little mouldy—my Willie diaries. As I read my almost indecipherable handwriting, suddenly the realisation came to me: I had found a treasure-trove. In the pages which I was turning over in my hands were the observations, almost instantly recorded, of and about a great man. Two tasks remained to me: the first was to have typed out the quickly written notes from all my diaries—the second was to fill in the abbreviations in the text and to link the notes together.

I knew Willie intimately for many years. I will try to present him with the accuracy of a ciné-camera taking shots of a subject who is unaware that his conversation and movements are being recorded. If some of the things he said were trivial, and if he often repeated himself, it must be remembered that towards the end he was a worn man. Inasmuch as this book has been compiled from my diaries, I will deliberately include the repetitions which occurred, because I want to give an honest picture of what he was like—particularly in his ageing years. I will try to complete—"warts and all"—the portrait of a famous man of letters.

*   *   *

Who *were* the Maughams, I used to ask Willie, and where did they come from? Willie said that he didn't care a tinker's cuss. But when the *Genealogists' Magazine* came out with an article called "Two Royal Descents" tracing our ancestry back to King Edward I, Willie was quite amused and interested.

"I'm *ter-terribly* impressed," he stammered. Then he looked up at me with a sarcastic smile. "But I daresay you've noticed that all the descents are in the female line," he added. "Didn't the Maughams have *any* reputable ancestors?"

Willie's great-great-great-grandfather was born in the reign of Charles II. He was a yeoman farmer in Westmorland—his house is still standing. He had eight children, one of whom was so respectable that he became a clergyman and a schoolmaster. This was the Reverend William Maugham, Master of the Free Grammar School at Moulton, in Lincolnshire, for fifty years until his death in 1814. I have an old box full of the Reverend William's sermons which he wrote out in longhand on pages cut to the size of a postcard and bound together with cotton. They are dull and staid. Sometimes a sermon was composed for a special occasion, such as Wolfe's victory at Quebec in 1759. But even Nelson's victory at Trafalgar in 1805 failed to inspire the man.

There is no foreshadowing of Willie's neat diamond-cut prose and stark realism in the whole bunch of his namesake's conventional sermons.

*   *   *

The youngest of the Westmorland farmer's eight children was named Robert, and he was Willie's great-great-grandfather. He was a glazier, who spent most of his life in the ancient town of Appleby, where he died in the year of Waterloo. But his sons came south to London to seek more genteel professions. There seems to have been almost a mass movement of Maughams away from Westmorland and the other Border counties in the late eighteenth and early nineteenth centuries. Some even emigrated to America—including a grandchild of the Reverend William, who bought a thirty-acre farm in Summit County, Ohio, for six hundred dollars.

Willie's great-grandfather was also called William. He was the eldest son of Robert the glazier, and he seems to have had some nodding acquaintance with the legal profession—perhaps as a clerk in a solicitor's office or in a firm of law stationers, for he was living in Chancery Lane when his first child was born in 1788. I wish I knew more about him. He must have had certain qualities to have produced a long line of lawyers and writers.

His eldest son, Robert, entered the employment of an attorney in Threadneedle Street. He worked as an ordinary clerk for some years and was given his articles in 1812. Apparently he was quite successful in practice, but he seems to have been more concerned with the well-being of the profession as a whole than for his own future. In 1825 he published his *Treatise on the Law of Attornies*, which was the first attempt to provide attorneys with a text-book covering every aspect of their professional activities. This "energetic little man" who became the "father of legal journalism"* was also one of the founders and the first secretary of the Law Society, with a salary of £400 a year and "apartments for his family in the newly completed Hall". In 1830 he founded the Legal Observer, "the first successful legal journal to combine current professional news with reports of cases and articles of practical interest to lawyers", and he continued as its proprietor and editor until 1856 when he sold out.

A Maugham had made good at last.

The portrait of Robert Maugham in the Law Society's hall shows an impressive-looking, rather sinister man with dark, piercing eyes and a firm jaw. And Robert seems to have had the Maugham temperament. When Willie was a boy he met an old solicitor who had dined in his youth at Robert Maugham's house.

"A servant handed the old party a dish of potatoes baked in their jackets," Willie told me. "But it seems that your great-grandfather didn't like them for some reason. Anyhow he took up the potatoes one by one and threw them at the pictures round the wall. And nobody dared say a word."

*　　　*　　　*

When Robert Maugham died in 1862, his eldest son, Robert Ormond Maugham—Willie's father—was already a well-established lawyer. He had his own firm in Paris and was also solicitor to the British Embassy. A year later he married Edith Mary Snell, whose mother, the widow of a major in the service of the East India Company, had settled in Paris to have her two daughters

* Mr Michael Birks in *The Law Society's Gazette* for December, 1959.

educated at a convent school. The old lady also had some talent as an author, and she wrote a dozen or so tales for French children, that were published in the series *Bibliothèque Morale de la Jeunesse*. It was through her, incidentally, that my uncle Willie and I derived our smart ancestors and our drop of Edward I's royal blood.

Edith Snell was twenty-three and very lovely when she married Robert Ormond Maugham.

"She was lovely, with russet hair, a straight little nose, and a creamy complexion, almost wax-like," I was told by her god-daughter, Mrs Hammersley.* "Her great brown eyes were always sad. She must have suffered a lot of pain from her terrible consumption, and she was sometimes terribly ill. My mother, who always took me visiting with her in the afternoons, often had tea with Mrs Maugham. Your grandmother would give me a doll to play with. I would take it with me under the tea-table. I could hear them above me, talking in low and earnest tones."

---

* Violet Williams-Freeman, later Mrs Arthur Hammersley, was a god-daughter of Edith Maugham, Willie's mother and, like Willie, had been born in the British Embassy in Paris. A friend of many of the Bloomsberries—Lytton Strachey, Desmond MacCarthy, Duncan Grant and Virginia Woolf; a family friend of the Mitfords—Mrs Hammersley, whom I met in 1963, died on Willie's ninetieth birthday—January 25th, 1964. Only that morning she had written to me. She stamped the letter, but she never posted it. Her solicitors found it and sent it on to me. It was quite a short letter, lively yet muddled, but I was able to make out the first few lines. "Dear Robin," she wrote, "I feel I must write you a line because on every page of every paper which passes through my hands I am faced with photographs of Willie, and dissertations about him—his dignity, benignity, deep loving kindness—until I scarcely feel I ever knew my faithful friend at all ... And yet I'm sure I did ..."

I reminded Mrs Hammersley that my grandparents had been known as "Beauty and the Beast" by their friends.

"Oh yes," she replied. "Your grandfather was very ugly—almost a monster to look at, with a large, very yellow face and very yellow eyes. But he was a very loving parent, and wonderfully kind to children."

The Maughams moved in a brilliant circle of friends in Paris. To their large and spacious apartment on the third floor of number 25 Avenue d'Antin (now Avenue Franklin D. Roosevelt) might come Prosper Mérimée and Gustave Doré and Clemenceau, together with some of the most influential and talented people of their day.

Charles Ormond, their first son, was born in November 1865. Frederic Herbert, my father, was born in October 1866, and their third son Henry Neville, called Harry, was born in 1868. My grandmother was frail and suffered from tuberculosis, but child-bearing was believed at that time to be helpful in combating the disease. Her first three sons flourished and her fourth son, William Somerset Maugham, was born on January 25th, 1874. But the next child was still-born. And in January 1882, wasted and exhausted, Willie's mother died, at the age of forty-one, after bearing yet another child, which lived for only a few hours.

*   *   *

Willie adored his mother, and for most of the five years after his eldest brothers had been packed off to school at Dover College in 1877, he had her warm affection all to himself. He was shattered by her death.

But the death of his mother and his stammer were not the only afflictions that Willie had to bear when he was a boy. He had been brought up to believe that his family was rich. His mother and father had lived in a grand style. Even at the time of his wife's death, Robert Maugham was building an expensive country house outside Paris. But when Robert died it was discovered that the family's wealth existed only in his imagination. Robert left little money behind him, and his children suddenly found that they were poor. Charles, the eldest son, succeeded his father in the Paris firm, assisted at times by Harry. My father only managed to get to Cambridge because he won two scholarships, and there was only just enough money to pay for Willie's education. The social position in which he now found himself was an added humiliation to Willie's life. In Paris, every luxury had been available; in Whitstable, where Willie had been sent to live with his uncle in the Vicarage, the vicar and his wife scraped carefully and constantly to make ends meet. In Paris, famous and titled people had attended his mother's salon; in Whitstable, Willie was ashamed to see his uncle toadying to the local squire.

"He was a vulgar lout who would never have been tolerated in my mother's drawing-room," Willie told me. "I wrote my novel *Of Human Bondage* to rid myself of an intolerable obsession," Willie said. "I wanted to lay all those ghosts, and I succeeded."

But did he succeed? I don't think so.

I believe those early years were a crucial influence in Willie's life. They affected him permanently both in important and trivial ways. To take the less important first; in Paris, after his mother's death, Willie, who had been brought up to speak French, was taught English by an English clergyman attached to the British Embassy. This clergyman, who must have been rather strange, taught the eight-year-old boy English by making him read aloud the police-court reports in the London newspapers. Willie learned about the murky side of life at an early age, and the fact that French was the first language he spoke left an impression on his style.

The early years moulded Willie's character. The humiliation of watching his uncle's toadying to the local squire made Willie relish friendship with the great, the titled and the affluent later in his life. It was a compensation for the years when he was poor and felt himself disdained. To the end of his days he loved to tell stories about rich and powerful acquaintances, about celebrities or royalty.

At the Villa Mauresque, Willie told me of a neighbour of his who heard that a newcomer to the Riviera, a woman whose husband had recently died, had acquired a villa on Cap Ferrat.

"My neighbour was informed that this woman was extremely rich," Willie said, clasping and unclasping his hands as he sometimes did when telling a story. "Extremely rich. But my neighbour was quite indignant.

" 'Nonsense,' he replied. 'Pure nonsense. I happen to know that she wasn't left more than thirty million.'

"You see," Willie explained to me, "though I'm a millionaire, compared to some of my neighbours here on the Cap, I'm a *very poor* millionaire... One of my neighbours is so rich that he practically controls the whole French government," Willie continued.

Two more stories may help to illustrate my point.

Willie once complained that a female visitor to the Mauresque had failed to admire his pictures.

"Why should you care that she didn't admire them?" a friend asked.

"Because they cost a lot of money," Willie replied.

On another occasion a young man was lunching at the

Mauresque for the first time. Towards the end of the meal Willie suddenly turned to him.

"You may think you're eating gruel," Willie said. "But it is *zabaglione*—and very expensive to make."

The poor young man was speechless.

*   *   *

But the most important influence on Willie's life was his stammer. Writing about his friend Arnold Bennett's stammer, Willie said: "Few knew the humiliations it exposed him to . . . and the minor exasperation of thinking of a good, amusing or apt remark and not venturing to say it in case the stammer ruined it. Few knew the distressing sense it gave rise to of a bar to complete contact with other men. It may be that except for the stammer which forced him to introspection Arnold would never have become a writer."

It is probable that if he had lost his stammer Willie would not have been an agnostic; it is almost certain that without his stammer Willie would not have been a writer; he would probably have become a lawyer—like his brothers. Willie's stammer made him reserved; it forced him to remain an onlooker; it made him into the detached observer of life who became the first person singular of his writing. His stammer made his prose pithy, crisp and succinct. His stammer made the dialogue of his plays neatly turned and well-balanced. Perhaps his impediment made his fame.

*   *   *

I seldom met Willie when I was a child but I can remember that he invited me to lunch at the Savoy when I was seven or eight. And I ordered oysters, which were a special supplement.

"You would be unlike the rest of your family if you did not prefer the most expensive," Willie told me.

My childhood memories of him were of a neatly dressed, attractive man with skin the colour of parchment, who sometimes visited the nursery. I got to know more about him when I was seventeen, and it was decided that I should go to Vienna. My darling sister Kate was to accompany me for the first two weeks.

A few days before I left England, when I went down to breakfast in the large, dank family house in Cadogan Square, I could see from my father's face that something had gone wrong.

"Such a meeting would be highly unsuitable," my father was saying to my mother. "The man's a drunkard and worse."

"Then Robin needn't meet him if you don't want him to," my mother replied.

"But the man's staying in the same hotel," my father said reproachfully.

Later I found out what had occurred. My uncle Willie had written a letter to my father saying he was delighted to hear that I was going to Vienna because Gerald Haxton, his American secretary, was already there, staying at the Koenig von Ungarn.

"Robin and Kate must change their hotel," my father decided.

So Kate and I went to a different hotel with severe instructions never to meet the infamous Gerald Haxton. But we did meet him—quite by chance, the very first night we went to the Opera. And I was disappointed, for he didn't look wicked at all: he was a smart, dapper lean man of forty with a small moustache, a cheerful laugh, and an innocent smile.

But after two weeks, Kate left me in Vienna, and one

evening Gerald took me round the town and got drunk in a *weinstube*. I then realised that he was not quite as innocent as he seemed. As he drank coffee laced with brandy, he began to talk about Willie. I found I could understand his slurred sentences, and gradually I began to understand the story of their relationship.

"When the First World War broke out, your uncle took a job as an interpreter with the Red Cross," Gerald told me. "He was an excellent interpreter but his shyness and stammer—quite apart from his upper-class accent—made it difficult for him to get through to the troops.

"I first saw him at a hospital in France, where I was an orderly. He was trying to cope with a Cockney soldier who'd been badly wounded in the stomach and was crying out for water, which the doctors had forbidden him to drink. I recognised Willie because of course he was already famous and I'd seen his photograph in the papers, with four plays running in London.

" 'I'm sorry, but is there anything else I can do to help?' your uncle was saying. 'Can I write a letter home for you?'

" 'Raite a lettah?' the soldier was saying in a ghastly imitation of Willie's accent, 'Not on your life.'

"I thought the time had come for me to intervene, so I breezed up and gave the soldier a cigarette, told him a few dirty stories, and soon had him grinning through his pain.

"The hospital was in an old Château which had been taken over. That night Willie and I were standing together on the terrace. We were looking down on the lawns that rolled gently towards a lake shimmering in the moonlight.

" 'Why can't you talk to them?' I asked Willie. 'Why can't you get through?'

" 'Because I'm shy and because I stammer,' he replied.

" 'What do you want in life,' I asked him, 'when this is over?'

" 'I want to travel and I want to be the most successful writer alive,' he smiled at me. 'That's all,' he concluded.

" 'You'll never be a world-famous writer if you can't get through to your raw material,' I told him. Mark you, I can't remember my exact words, but I can recall the general drift of the conversation because it was to make all the difference to my life.

" 'What do *you* want?' he asked me.

" 'From you or from life?'

" 'Perhaps both,' he answered. 'They might turn out to be the same thing.'

" 'You see, what I want is fun and games,' I told him, 'but I've not got a cent. So I want someone to look after me and give me clothes and parties. And the odd thing is that I reckon I could give you what you are after as well if I were your friend. If you took me on your travels I'd be the one who picked up the interesting character in a low bar and got a story for you.'

"I can remember that Willie was silent for a moment.

" 'Perhaps you could,' he answered."

Gerald ordered himself another cognac.

"Later," he continued, "we went up to my room where I had a bottle of gin." Gerald smiled to himself. "And that's how it all began," he told me.

A few weeks later Willie was sent back to England.

"They wanted him for Intelligence, but I didn't know that at the time," said Gerald. "When he came to say good-bye to me I told him that I was getting fed-up with my hospital work and I wanted to get back to America. 'I don't reckon I'll stick it here for long without you,' I said. 'I'll find my way back to New York. But we must meet again somehow.'

" 'You needn't worry about the future,' Willie said quietly.

" 'Without a cent?' I asked him.

" 'You needn't worry, Gerald,' he told me, 'because I'll look after you.' And he has, more or less, ever since."

For a while Gerald stared at a young boy in *lederhosen*. Then he turned to me.

"The trouble was that Willie had determined to persuade himself that he was a complete heterosexual," Gerald said, "And that's why he'd got tangled up with Syrie Wellcome. She was a clever, scheming person, and she knew how to handle Willie. By the time he'd realised the truth about her it was too late, he'd married her and they had produced a child. I knew he'd divorce her, and I knew he'd come back to me in time, because I'd helped him get his stories. It was I who would stay up late in the club in some place like Penang and would get pally with planters and lawyers. I'd get them drunk and they would tell me stories, such as *The Letter*, which I got for Willie from a lawyer in Singapore. And I got dozens more apart from that. Besides, married life didn't suit Willie—he was far happier when he was with me. He enjoyed our travels in the Far East. He loved our adventures in places such as Tahiti. And the stories he wrote were a tremendous success. They made his name as a serious writer as well as being a successful dramatist. He's now the most famous writer alive, and I suppose I ought to be grateful that I'm his friend and secretary. The Mauresque is a very beautiful house and I'm sure that Willie is very proud of it."

Gerald ordered himself another brandy. By now he was very drunk.

"I like it most days," Gerald continued. "But at times when I'm shut up there in that great villa all alone with him I feel I could scream. He has moods when he gets depressed; I wonder sometimes if he isn't haunted. His face looks sad and grim. But then he'll say something to make me smile, or to fascinate me, and I will forgive him everything . . . I've had too much to drink, and I know it. But there are moments when I wonder if in order to get all his success and money he's had to sell his soul to the devil. You know that he was pals with Aleister Crowley? You must have heard of Aleister Crowley."

"Yes," I answered, "wasn't he the man who went in for black magic?"

"That's the one," Gerald replied. "People think that Aleister Crowley was an old fraud. But I know better. And sometimes I wonder if he didn't come to Willie and say, 'If you give me your soul I'll make you the most famous writer alive in this century.' And I believe that somehow Willie accepted."

I met Gerald frequently during his stay in Vienna and I came to believe that his attitude towards Willie was schizophrenic. At one moment he'd tell me how much he loved Willie and what a great man Willie was and how vast was his fame and success; a minute later he'd be raging against Willie and complaining of being a prisoner when he was in the Mauresque.

*   *   *

That summer I stayed in a *pension* by the lake at Klopeinersee. I was there when Dolfuss was assassinated. A Nazi putsch was expected at any moment. My mother's brother, General Sir Cecil Romer, who was Deputy Chief of Imperial General Staff, telephoned her to say there was a danger of war. My mother sent me a telegram asking me to return to England, but I decided to spend a few more days by the lake before leaving Austria.

I was sunbathing, half-asleep on the shore, when to my amazement I heard my uncle's voice.

"There's the young man," Willie said. "How beautifully brown he is."

I turned round. Gerald Haxton was standing beside Willie.

"We've come to rescue you," Gerald announced. "We're taking you to Bad Gastein and then putting you on a 'plane for England."

"Go and pack," Willie said to me, "I want to be back in Bad Gastein in time for dinner."

We drove away from Klopeinersee in Willie's lovely Voisin. It was a long drive. Willie and Gerald began to talk about music. After a while I felt I must chip in with some remark.

"I think Bach's music is rather mechanical," I said. "You can almost guess what's coming next."

Willie turned to me.

"That," he said, "is the kind of remark that eighteen-year-olds make to try and sound impressive."

"But Robin *is* eighteen," Gerald pointed out.

"I dare say," Willie answered, "but all the same the remark is completely puerile and displays his ignorance of music." Then he turned back to me.

"Don't look so depressed," he murmured. "I only said what I did because I don't want you to grow up saying more than you understand."

That evening in Bad Gastein after we'd eaten blinis and blue trout, Gerald got up from the table and said he was going to the casino. I was left alone with Willie. Presently he leaned towards me, and I could see that he intended to say something of importance. I took a gulp of hock.

"I would like, if I mer-may, to give you a word of

advice," Willie stammered. "You are quite an attractive boy. Don't waste your assets. Your charm won't last for long."

With those words he left the table.

*   *   *

I visited the Mauresque in the summer of 1936. I was surprised by Willie's kindness. He would take me for walks around Cap Ferrat, and he would make me see the umbrella pines, the inlets and the enchanting landscapes in a way which at that time I could not envisage for myself. He was so relaxed and friendly that I felt I could say or ask him anything.

"When you were my age," I said to him, "were you ever in love with some boy or girl of your own age?"

"Yes," Willie replied. "Quite frequently."

"And at times was your love unrequited?"

"Most certainly."

"But then how did you get over it?" I asked.

"I'd look at the boy I was in love with, and I'd think to myself: 'One day your face will be as lined as your father's is, and your hair will be grey and balding and you'll have a paunch-belly and there'll be not a trace left of the beautiful slim youth that you are today.' "

"But thinking that wouldn't help me at all," I said. "It depresses me horribly to think that a young boy will one day be an obese old man. And that's what makes unrequited love so painful to me—because I feel that every day my loved-one is growing older and must inevitably in time be decayed."

"The thought of dissolution depresses you because you are still young, and you're a romantic by nature."

"But what is the point of it all?" I asked.

23

Willie stopped walking and stood for a moment, gazing out at the sea.

"If there is any point—which I sometimes doubt," he said, "surely it must be to make a good shape of one's life . . . with its beginning, its middle and its end . . . so that it makes a complete and perfect pattern—like the perfect play I've always wanted to write. Or so I believe. But it's a difficult ambition to achieve because many of the events that shape our lives are beyond our control. For instance, Otho Stuart, who was a famous manager in his day, had run into a difficulty with a play at the Royal Court Theatre, Sloane Square, and he wanted a replacement so that the theatre shouldn't be dark. Aleister Crowley, one of my disreputable friends, introduced me to him. Now I'd just written a play called *Lady Frederick*. You may have seen one of the revivals. It's about a middle-aged woman of fashion who lives by her wits. A young peer is in love with her. In the last act she decides to disillusion him. She has him invited to her dressing-room at the Hotel de Paris, Monte Carlo, and she lets him see her without her make-up. Now Otho Stuart doubted that there was any leading actress in those days who would appear in front of her public without make-up on. As it happened, he found one; Ethel Irving, and the play went on. I was terrified the first night. Your mother told me afterwards that I looked as if I was going to faint, I was so pale and trembling. I shall never forget when the curtain rose on the last act where the leading actress has to come in through the curtains from her bedroom wearing a kimono. Her hair was all dishevelled, hanging about her head in a tangled mop. She wasn't made up; she looked haggard and yellow and lined. In fact she looked ghastly. There was a gasp of amazement from the audience, then complete silence which lasted

24

till the end of the scene with the young peer who had come to visit her. The audience were completely held as she put on her make-up at her dressing-table in front of her young lover, who looked at her aghast. The curtain fell to rapturous applause. I shall never forget the sound of it.

"There was a first-night party at the Bath Club in London that night. The cast and various celebrities were present. I wish I could make you see the scene. The ladies were all in full evening dress; the men were in white ties and tails. I stood there with my arm linked with Ethel Irving. We were in the centre of an admiring group. Suddenly the doors at the end of the room were thrown open and my brother Harry appeared. Harry had also adopted the profession of literature but he wrote long plays in blank verse at a time when they were unpopular. He was praised by some critics but the public didn't appreciate him at all.

"At a glance I could see that Harry had been drinking. He was wearing a shabby lounge suit. There was a moment of complete silence. Then Harry spoke in a loud, ringing voice.

" 'I'm glad to hear that my little brother has had some success at last,' he said.

"It was an awkward moment. But it didn't alter the fact that the play was a triumphant success. I was now a celebrity and invited to all kinds of smart parties. But if *Lady Frederick* had failed—and I think it would have done if Ethel Irving had not consented to play the part— I'd made up my mind that I would give up writing as a career and I'd sign on as a ship's doctor. After all, I'd qualified as a doctor, which was how I came to write *Liza of Lambeth*. The novel outraged your dear father, and even startled your dear mother somewhat. And I suppose I might never have been heard of again.

25

"I tell you the story to show that we can only shape our lives to a certain extent, but at least one can try."

*　　　*　　　*

When I was staying at the Mauresque on that occasion the only other guest in the villa was Barbara Back. She was married to the well-known surgeon, Ivor Back, who was too busy to visit the Riviera. After Willie had divorced Syrie and had bought the Mauresque to live there with Gerald, Barbara was a frequent guest during all the years that followed. Her vitality and quick wit delighted Willie. During his later years when there was a grand party to which distinguished people such as the Windsors or the Queen of Spain were invited, Barbara would act as hostess. Even when she was an elderly woman, her zest never failed, nor did her caustic tongue. She remained friends with Willie until the end of his life.

Another woman who was a close friend of Willie's was G. B. Stern, the popular novelist known to her friends as Peter. She would sometimes accompany Willie and Gerald on their trips in Europe. She was full of good conversation and vitality but I do not think it was these qualities which attracted Willie to her. Willie liked having women around him for two reasons. First, because they lent him confidence. Perhaps in some small way they could make up for the death of his mother. But there was a second reason. Willie was still determined that only a minor part of his character was homosexual, and he took great care to conceal it from his public. Thus he never wrote a homosexual novel as such, although the discerning reader can detect a trace of homosexuality in his excellent novel *The Narrow Corner*. With Peter Stern, Willie adopted the position of facetious lover.

"Peter, my sweet," he would begin a letter to her. "I

am so sorry you are sick . . . and though you don't ask *me*
I shall come to your door and crave admittance. Not 'arf.
Willie."

"Peter, my Peter," his letters would begin, or "Delilah,
you are irresistible, as you well know—and who can fail
to succumb to your wiles, even though one may know that
one's end will be eyeless in Gaza."

Or "Precious, post-prandial Peter," or "My very dear
little Peter" or "Blessed Among Women" or "My precious
Peter Petrovina".

But though his letters were gay and facetious, there ran
through them a strain of genuine affection. Peter amused
Willie and her obvious love for him was welcome to him.
But his friendship for Barbara lasted longer, and when
Peter—because of her ill-health—had sold her rooms in
Albany, Piccadilly, and had retired to a cottage in the
country, Willie seldom saw her. He seemed able to forget
friends when they were no longer useful to him.

*   *   *

Barbara Back was graceful, elegant, unceasingly
entertaining and unusually detached. I knew from both
Willie and Gerald that although Barbara was happily
married with a son of about my own age, she was one of
their favourite companions. Willie had known Barbara
for years and had hinted to me that Syrie had been a
little jealous of the close friendship he shared with
Barbara.

Barbara was a brave woman—but she was terrified of
mosquitoes. There were so many mosquitoes on Cap
Ferrat that we slept under nets. When I was staying at
the Mauresque, I slept in the room next to that which
was occupied by Barbara. I think it may have been
because I rescued her from a mosquito which had

penetrated the nets covering her bed that we first became friends.

"I can't sleep tonight," Barbara told me. "Bring up a chair and let's talk."

Barbara was one of those rare individuals with whom it was possible to feel close kinship almost upon meeting. Soon what had started out as a casual late-night conversation became more intimate. There was much I longed to know about my uncle's life; Barbara as an old and close friend of his knew the answers to a lot of the questions that I wanted to ask. Willie's divorce from Syrie had taken place when I was ten; but the story fascinated me. How had Willie—whom I knew to be homosexual—come to marry? "How did he first meet Syrie?" I asked Barbara.

"Perhaps it was inevitable they should meet," Barbara told me. "We all moved in the same circles in those days so Willie and Syrie were bound to coincide one day. But, as it happens, they met rather by accident. Some neighbour or other of Willie's had arranged a small theatre party and at the last moment one of the men dropped out. The neighbour asked Willie—very much at the last minute—if he would make up the numbers. Over dinner before the theatre Willie found he was acting as escort to Mrs Syrie Wellcome." Barbara paused for a moment.

"What happened?" I asked.

"Well, by all accounts, Syrie made a dead set at Willie," Barbara continued. "After all, he was rather a celebrity —one of the most successful playwrights of the day."

I remembered that at the time of their meeting both Willie and Syrie had been mature people—Willie had been in his late thirties; Syrie was a little younger.

"You know, I ought to have been a journalist," Barbara said. "I have the most amazing memory. Of course, when

I can't remember *exactly* what happened, I always use my imagination. Now, what were we saying?"

"What were Willie and Syrie like together?" I asked.

"I can remember a particular party we were all at," Barbara continued. "The party was in Mayfair, in Chesterfield Street in a house which belonged to some people called Dennison. He was as rich as Croesus and she was quite a fashionable hostess at that time. I was beginning to get bored when, to my joy, Willie appeared. He asked me where my husband was, and I told him that he had an operation to do. I told Willie that he was looking rather tired. 'I am tired,' Willie said. 'I'm exhausted, in fact.'

" 'Well, I suppose you'll have to make up your mind,' I said to him.

" 'About what, precisely?' he asked.

" 'About what you want,' I told him. 'You see, I'd say that part of you relishes your fame and all this fashionable hoo-ha. But part of you disapproves because it interferes with your work.'

" 'You're not only attractive, my dear Barbara,' Willie told me, 'you are also intelligent.' At that moment Willie noticed Syrie and Henry Wellcome arriving. Wellcome was a successful chemist, twenty years older than Syrie, and shortly to be knighted. Syrie, as I'm sure you are aware, was the daughter of the Victorian philanthropist Dr Barnardo. I could see that Willie was unusually interested in her. By this time she was exchanging pleasantries with old Dennison—so I went over and brought her across to join us."

"But how," I asked, "how did it happen?"

"Well, I've told you that from the first Syrie had made a dead set for Willie—and he was patently obviously very flattered by her interest. There was a strong attraction there for both of them—and without saying that Willie was totally ruthless, I may add that there is a vast difference between being in love with a married woman and being in love with one who is completely unattached. That summer before the war seemed to be incredibly beautiful, a perfect summer. Willie, I remember, was planning to go off to Capri later—he shared a villa there with Dodo Benson*—and Syrie was planning to join him there later. Anyway, it was very much apparent there was a strong attraction between them."

"Were they in love?" I asked.

"It's difficult to say. Yes, probably," Barbara replied. "It was hot in that drawing-room so we wandered out on to the balcony. I was chatting away with Syrie—but I noticed that Willie was quite silent. Of course, in those days his stammer made him shy. Syrie asked him what he was thinking about.

" 'I was reflecting about my betters,' Willie told her, gesturing towards the ballroom, 'inside there.'

" '*Our* betters,' Syrie corrected. 'I don't really belong in this set—although I suppose I could if I really wanted to.'

" '*Our* betters,' Willie repeated. 'It would make quite a good title for a play.'

"Syrie told Willie that she had seen all his plays and that she had loved all of them. Willie was naturally flattered. 'I needed to hear praise tonight,' he said. 'I was beginning to think my plays were just trivial and shallow.'

"Syrie insisted they were not. This pleased Willie. Syrie was looking particularly radiant that night, and Willie's eyes hardly left her face. 'You're a novelist and a

* "Dodo" Benson; the nickname given to novelist and biographer E. P. Benson—author of the Mapp and Lucia novels and of society novels featuring a hostess called Dodo, based upon Margot Asquith.

dramatist as well, so I should think you could tell my character at a glance,' Syrie said, conscious that Willie was intently examining her.

" 'Not just at a glance,' Willie said. 'However, I can tell you one thing. You're like crême brulée. Brittle on the surface but unexpectedly soft beneath it.'

"Syrie laughed. 'And am I a faithful person, would you say?'

"Willie suddenly became very serious. 'To your husband? I hope not. To a friend? Faithful? Yes . . . I'd say unusually so.'

"I decided to chip in. I told Syrie that her husband had left the party about half an hour earlier—from our vantage point on the balcony I'd seen him departing. It seemed like a good time for me to leave too; I was feeling hot, sticky and tired. But Willie suggested the three of us should drive out to Richmond, saying it would be cool and pleasant out there. I protested tiredness—but both of them made such a fuss, insisted that I accompany them. In the end I gave in and went with them. You see, I think that the two of them were still in some odd sort of way a bit shy of being left alone together. So I gave in gracefully and off we drove to Richmond. I can remember we sat on a bench at the top of the stairs which lead to the eighteenth-century pagoda. The park was gleaming in the moonlight. It was a divine evening. We were silent for a while; I felt slightly uncomfortable—as if I were intruding.

"Syrie suddenly asked Willie why he had decided to become a writer. Willie's answer was particularly interesting. 'If I could tell you why,' he said, 'I'd be a great writer—instead of somewhere near the top of the second league.'

"Syrie insisted that Willie would be a great writer;

she was quite emphatic about it. It surprised me so much that I asked her how she could be so sure. 'Because that's what he wants most in the world,' she told me. 'I believe if one wants something strongly enough, one gets it.'

"But Willie disagreed with her. 'It's *not* what I want most in the world,' he said. 'I want something far simpler yet far more difficult to get. I want what every man yearns for—however stupid or however clever he may be, however rich or however poor.' "

Barbara lapsed into silence.

"What was it?" I asked.

Barbara thought for a moment. "You know, I've often pondered on it and have never quite been able to make up my mind. I think perhaps that what Willie wanted most in the world was something far simpler than riches and success—though they are tremendously important to him. I think that what he craved most in the world was happiness."

Barbara paused for a while, as if lost in thought. " 'People think you're a cynic,' Syrie said to Willie. 'But at heart you're a pure romantic . . . Do you know, this is a moment I've always imagined. Not here—it was always in the country; never London. This is the moment, and now it's happened.'

"I decided that the time had come for me to leave the two of them alone together. I stood up and told them I was going to take a stroll. They didn't try to stop me."

*   *   *

The following morning I found Barbara sitting by the swimming-pool. She greeted me warmly and we began to talk again. "Did Willie ever really love Syrie?" I asked.

"Yes," Barbara answered. "I'm certain of it. You must remember that she was rather beautiful—a real glamour puss. She was small and pretty, with radiant brown eyes and a beautiful skin. Syrie had high spirits and was endowed with a brilliant vivacity. And of course she lived in a very smart set which—in those days—impressed Willie. You see he didn't at all mind being known as Syrie's lover. In fact, he was rather proud of it. Then came trouble. The first thing was that Henry Wellcome, who by now, I think, had been knighted, decided that he wasn't going to put up with the situation any longer. He decided to institute proceedings for divorce—citing Willie as co-respondent. Willie was appalled. Syrie had always said that she and Wellcome had a separation agreement by which she could do as she pleased. She had always said that Wellcome didn't mind at all. But, of course, he did. Syrie broke the news to Willie, and there was an hysterical scene in which she said he must marry her. Now being the lover of a smart hostess and being married were two very different things. Willie evaded the issue as best he could. From that moment on things began to go wrong." Barbara paused for a moment. "You know, at that time Willie was working on *Of Human Bondage*," she continued. "Syrie simply didn't understand how important his writing was to Willie. She would try to get him to take her to Henley or some such place when he wanted the morning completely to himself. What's more, Syrie didn't approve of what she'd read of the novel. She found it sad and squalid. She told Willie it would never be a bestseller. Of course, she was right in a way. Because when the book came out in England in 1915, I think it was, it didn't have awfully good reviews and didn't sell particularly well. But the American critics and the American public were much more enthusiastic. You could say that the man who writes those very long and very dull novels, Theodore Dreiser, *made* the book in America. His name carried great weight, and in his review he praised the book to the skies.

"Now I'll tell you something which may surprise you. Willie was—and is—a haunted man, and I've never been able to find out what it is that haunts him. Of course he was very uncertain about marriage—to say the least of it. He didn't think he was cut out to be a good husband—and he wasn't. But the war came along and gave him an excuse to get himself time to think things over. He joined up as a driver and a dresser in a Red Cross ambulance unit. And while he was in France . . . along came a young American orderly; Gerald. Willie was then forty, Gerald was in his early twenties and extremely handsome. The rest of the story you know.

"But, you see," Barbara continued, "even before he'd left England Willie had already begun to quarrel with Syrie. I'd witnessed some very irritable scenes. For example, I can remember after one party Willie had persuaded me to stay on for a night-cap. I told Syrie that I thought the party had been a great success. 'You didn't look too pleased about it,' Syrie said to Willie.

" 'I'm sorry,' Willie said. 'Ber-but I simply cannot stay up night after night at parties and work the next morning.' It was obvious that Syrie's nerves were on edge. 'Do you suppose the parties we give *don't* help your work? They've made you the best known author in England.'

" 'And they've made you one of the best known decorators in London,' Willie answered. 'What's wrong with that?' Syrie demanded. 'Nothing—so far as you're concerned,' Willie replied. 'But I'd rather be less well known and write better. So *you* go on giving parties, and *I'll* gladly pay for them. But I shan't be there.'

" 'How can I give parties without you?' Syrie asked. 'You can say I'm ill,' Willie answered, winking at me.

34

This really annoyed Syrie. 'You're being very selfish,' she told him.

" 'Is it selfish of me not to want to waste away my energy and talent?' Willie demanded. 'Can't you see how trivial our life is?' This didn't please Syrie at all. 'We know some of the most interesting people in town,' she stated. 'Is that so trivial?'

" 'Yes,' Willie replied, 'if we only know them trivially. I am tired of the hectic social existence we lead.' Then suddenly Willie's nerves snapped. 'I'm bored, do you hear me?' he shouted at her. 'I'm bored to distraction.'

"Syrie was close to tears. 'If we were married it would all be different,' she muttered. 'Ber-but it might be worse,' Willie said grimly. Then along came the war, and along came Gerald, as I've already told you . . . You know he's a strange man, your uncle. On one occasion quite recently he arrived at my front door in London in a taxi. It was pouring with rain. I opened the door myself as I was expecting him. 'I want threepence change,' Willie said.

" 'Your meanness will be the death of you,' I told him. At which point he came into the house and handed me an ermine coat. He's a curious one, your uncle. One never knows what to expect next. Perhaps that's why I'm so fond of him."

"But he married Syrie in New York, in 1916, after he'd left France and was in Intelligence," I said. "I know all that. How he went to Russia almost immediately after the marriage, on some secret mission. Then he came back with tuberculosis. I know that part of it. But how did the final break with Syrie occur?"

Barbara sighed. "Ah, well," she said. "I suppose it was inevitable. I happen to have been present at the actual occasion. It took place in Le Touquet—at Syrie's villa. The villa was designed and built by Syrie with her own

35

money. Willie did not contribute a penny towards it. Syrie built the villa. Perhaps it was her last hope of getting Willie back—and her last attempt at accepting Gerald. Mind you, I don't think Willie had the slightest intention of having her accept Gerald. But I don't really know, because I wasn't on those sort of terms with the two of them at the time. Syrie knew Willie would not live in England because Gerald wasn't allowed in—he had been pushed out by the Home Office after a very squalid law case.* Anyhow, she built the villa to make it possible for him to live there with her and with Gerald. The villa was long and white and set in pine trees—not much view, and not near the sea. There was a terrace, Syrie's room on the ground floor, with living-rooms and so on. Willie and Gerald had rooms upstairs. My room was downstairs."

"What year was this?" I asked.

"Oh, about 1926, I would suppose," Barbara said. "I don't think Syrie left me at Le Touquet alone with Gerald and Willie out of malice. Although my visit had been arranged for some time beforehand, it suited her to go to Paris at that particular moment. Perhaps she thought, 'Better than nobody, they can have Barbara.' She had told me such awful things about Willie and Gerald; she had also told me a number of times that Willie disliked Ivor and me. Therefore it never entered her head that we three would hit it off. When she returned to Le Touquet from Paris, she was as friendly with me as usual.

"Syrie asked me to go and stay with her at Le Touquet because she was preparing to have a try at accepting Gerald. When I arrived, and got out of the train, waiting for me on the platform was Willie—and the other man with him I knew must be Gerald. There was no sign of Syrie.

* See page (43).

"I was absolutely appalled. I had no idea Syrie would not be there; I wouldn't have come had I known she'd be away. She had left the villa to go to Paris on some business to do with her decorating. I was upset to discover I was left alone with Willie and Gerald and Willie's daughter Liza. Gerald I had never seen before, but I had heard from Syrie that he was the monster-of-the-world. Liza was an adorable child and Willie doted on her.

" 'I'm afraid you'll have to put up with Gerald and me,' Willie said. 'We'll try not to bore you.' I thought: 'Blast Syrie, I'll kill her for this.' Until then I had thought Syrie was a friend of mine. I was silent, too shaken to think of anything to say. But later on, after a delicious lunch at the villa, everything became fine. When we arrived at the villa Willie said, 'One of the things we are going to do is have tennis lessons—I shall stand everyone tennis lessons.' There were some tennis courts in the town. So we went for tennis lessons, and within twenty-four hours Gerald and I had become friends, and I had no more fear of Willie.

"Liza was a sweet little girl running about the place with her Nanny. We were all very happy.

" 'I der-don't like the casino,' Willie said to me, 'but I do like playing bridge. Can you find a fourth?' So Gerald and I drove to the casino and found a fourth. A girl called Laura Royston. Laura was the wife of Roy Royston, the actor. She was a very gay girl and used to come up in the evenings to make a fourth at bridge.

"Then Syrie arrived back from Paris. I am not sure whether she arrived with Frankie Leveson or whether he came from England on his own. He had been a ballroom dancer previously. He was a small, thin gigolo-type of man. Very tiny—he used to teach the Prince of Wales

37

dancing. When he died, Rex Evans said, 'Have you heard, Syrie's sent Frankie Leveson a pickled* coffin?'

"Beverley Nichols arrived at about the same time or just after their arrival, and also a Mrs Phillipson who owned a wonderful house at Sandgate. She pickled everything and it was from her that Syrie learned to pickle. She was a bit fey. She wasn't staying at the house; she just came from somewhere to lunch. One day she came to lunch and told a lovely story about meeting a dead man in the street. While it was going on, Beverley was sitting at the table, stroking the pears and the peaches and the cruets.

" 'Weren't you ter-taught when you were young not to stroke the fruit?' Willie remarked.

"Beverley didn't like this at all; he was very red and embarrassed. After lunch Beverley took me for a long drive (He can't drive *now*, so heaven knows what it was like *then*.) He said how difficult the atmosphere was at the villa. But I was quite friendly with Syrie—and very friendly with Willie and Gerald.

"I can remember one incident. Syrie was deciding where to put two chairs. Gerald said, 'How would you like them over here in the corner?' Syrie flew at him. 'I am not going to take *your* advice,' she said. Those are not her exact words. She was far more bitter. Gerald didn't turn a hair. But there was an awkward afternoon for the rest of us.

"In the mornings I would come in for breakfast, and there would be Willie sitting in one of his Chinese dressing-gowns, with slits, having his breakfast, and

---

* Syrie was famous as an interior decorator on both sides of the Atlantic. It was she who introduced the off-white style and she was very keen on "pickling" furniture—that is, soaking furniture in brine to remove colour.

waiting for Syrie to send for him. He was never talkative at these times, and if one spoke to him he would just say 'Hmmm?' Willie was *terrified* of Syrie.

"Syrie had this downstairs bedroom off the large room where breakfast was served. Her maid would come in and tell Willie when Syrie was ready to see him. 'Madame has finished her breakfast, sir,' she would say. Willie and Syrie would argue together in her room. We could hear her shouts, but not everything that was said. 'Don't shout . . . please . . . don't embarrass me . . . I have friends in the house,' Willie would say. 'Don't *make me* a scene.' That was one of Willie's favourite phrases.

"But the final row was caused by the laundry bill of all things. There was no laundry maid, so the laundry had to be collected from everyone and sent to the laundry in town. I remember making a list of mine. The laundry bill was on my table in my room one day— I don't remember how much it was, but I paid it and never thought any more about it. Upstairs the laundry bills were being discussed by Willie and Gerald, and Frankie Leveson overheard them. Being Frankie Leveson he couldn't wait to tell Syrie what Willie had said.

"Willie was still fuming about it hours later. I think it was at about cocktail time that he finally erupted. 'It's per-perfectly monstrous,' I can remember him saying. And Gerald tried to calm him down. 'It may well be,' he said. 'But for heaven's sake, don't make a scene. I feel as if I'm living on the edge of a volcano as it is.' Willie then turned to me and asked if I'd been given a laundry bill. 'Yes,' I replied. 'And I've paid it.' But you're a guest in this house,' Willie said. 'I know,' I said. 'But the laundry was done in Le Touquet—so presumably some-one had to pay for it. I paid for mine like a lamb. I don't see what all the fuss is about.'

" 'Guests aren't usually asked to pay for their laundry,' Willie said. 'When I buy a villa on the Riviera, my dear Barbara, there'll be a laundry in the house itself, I can assure you. And a laundry maid.' And of course, there is. It had been decided that we would dine at the casino. And at that moment Syrie came into the room. Someone, I can't remember who, commented that she was looking divine. But she must have sensed the atmosphere. She noticed that one of the chairs had been moved. 'Who moved the armchair?' she asked. Gerald admitted that he had. 'Then would you mind putting it back?' Syrie said. Gerald made as if to rise. 'Sit down, Gerald,' Willie said. 'We moved the chair because it makes the room look more comfortable,' he continued, addressing Syrie.

" 'It doesn't,' she snapped. 'It makes the room look vulgar and suburban. Put the chair back, Gerald. *Now*, if you please.' Willie was *furious*. His voice positively trembled with rage. 'I imagined you'd *want* the place to look vulgar and suburban—since you run it as a boarding-house,' he told her.

"Syrie stared at him in fury. '*What* was that you said?' she demanded. Willie's voice seemed suddenly very cool and very detached—'I said you seem to run this place as a common boarding-house,' he repeated. 'Already your lodgers are made to pay for their laundry bills. Soon, I suppose, we'll get our weekly bills for our food and rent.'

"Syrie looked at him for a moment in a stricken silence. Then she turned and walked very quickly, very erect, from the room. 'Oh, Willie,' I said. 'Now you've torn it.'

"I could understand Syrie's point of view," Barbara continued. "She'd paid for the villa. She'd paid for the servants and all the food and drink. And she had never asked Willie to contribute a penny... And then he attacked her over those ridiculous laundry bills. But what

40

she couldn't understand was that if he hadn't attacked her over the laundry bills, it would have been over something else. She couldn't face the fact that Willie didn't love her any more . . . that Gerald had won. She could not understand that. She'd lost the battle. So she went to London to see her lawyers and then came back after we'd all gone and spent the rest of the summer with Liza. But, you know, she did threaten to cite Gerald in the divorce action. But the lawyers arranged satisfactory alimony and the divorce came through in 1927.

"When we realised that Syrie had gone, Gerald and Willie and I thought, 'What can we do?' I was due in Alassio in just under a week and Willie had no plans, because he had been intending to stay on longer at Syrie's villa. Gerald and Willie and I were left at Le Touquet for a few days—then I went to Italy. I can't say where Willie and Gerald went, but for several months no one knew where they were, except me, because they used to send me picture postcards.

"I came back from Italy, with Ivor. We stayed the night at Le Touquet on our way to England. We went into the casino and I saw Syrie with Frankie Leveson. I said, 'Syrie, how lovely.' I went towards her with my arms outstretched. She cut me dead. I was left with my arms in the air. I was shattered. I'd *no* wish to fight with Syrie. I was fond of her. I didn't think we were on bad terms until that moment. I discovered later that it was impossible to be friends with both Syrie and Willie at the same time; it had to be one or the other."

*   *   *

That afternoon Willie took me for a walk around Cap Ferrat. "I am per-pleased to see you've been getting on so

41

well with Barbara," he said. "She is one of my dearest friends and an adorable creature. I have the highest regard for her. But perhaps I should warn you that like all of us her memory is not infallible—and she's gifted with an extraordinarily lively imagination. In fact, I should take what she tells you with a pinch of salt."

However, I wasn't so sure. Willie's reticence about his past was—and still is—notorious.

*   *   *

Though Barbara was the only other guest staying at the Mauresque at the time, there were many other guests for lunch or dinner—Michael Arlen, Armenian by birth but more English than the English, saturnine and dapper, at that time a bestselling author of a series of novels about the Mayfair "smart" set, the most famous of which, *The Green Hat*, had been dramatised with Tallulah Bankhead; Osbert Sitwell, majestic, venerable and witty; Harold Nicolson, twinkling and benign and extremely friendly towards me; Peter Stern, happily effusive and loquacious; Robert Hitchens, who provided a link with Oscar Wilde—for it had been Hitchens who had anonymously published a scandalously successful novel about Wilde and "Bosie" Douglas, based upon information gathered from Douglas on a cruise up the Nile in the company of E. F. Benson—Max Beerbohm, an aged dandy, still wonderfully spritely, speaking in the accents of the 1890s and choosing each word as fastidiously as he chose each garment he wore, courtly but carrying only a vestige of his exquisite past; Arnold Bennett, a fellow stammerer and bestselling writer whom Willie had known since the turn of the century, in the days when they were both struggling in the Bohemian stews of Paris; H. G. Wells, a one-time neighbour in the South of France, with his squeaky voice and prophetical opinions, whom Willie in a memorial piece published after his death ten years later described as "a good man"; Beverley Nichols, smart, small and witty in a kind way.

As I have said elsewhere, the house seemed to be effortlessly run. It took me some time to realise that it was Gerald Haxton who was largely responsible for the atmosphere of happiness and comfort in which I was now living. Gerald's high spirits seemed to infect the whole villa, and he had a quality which I can only describe as "lift"—by which I mean that the vitality he exuded was so strong that it infected most people around him. Gerald's attitude towards me was perplexing. In Vienna he had made no secret of the fact that he wanted to go to bed with me, and I could see that he was still attracted to me. But he made no further approaches. It was a rule at the Mauresque that everyone should bathe naked in the swimming-pool, and as I would lie sun-bathing, if I suddenly looked up, I would find Gerald staring at me.

By now I knew more about Gerald than I had known when we were in Vienna—he was wayward, feckless and brave. He was also—from his days as a schoolboy—used to being admired. He was very spoilt. In these days he had begun to drink heavily; he would become wild and violent in his cups. His reputation was notorious, his behaviour was reckless. In the winter of 1915, when Gerald was in London, he was arrested on a charge of gross indecency. The case came up before Mr Justice Humphreys on December 7th, 1915, and he was acquitted by the jury. But the judge was convinced that Gerald was guilty of the office and made no secret of it. A few years later Gerald was declared an undesirable alien. He was never allowed to return to England again. This was one of the factors that decided Willie to live abroad.

43

Gerald always pretended that the reason he never accompanied Willie on his trips to London was because he loathed the place. But the cigarettes he smoked still came from Bond Street, his suits from his old tailor in Savile Row, and his shirts from Jermyn Street.

Another welcome guest at the Mauresque was Noël Coward. Willie delighted in the fortune he himself had amassed; he frequently contemplated and drew attention to the plight of authors who had failed on the road to success or fallen by the wayside. This concern with their misfortune led to his generous gifts and bequests to such societies as might benefit struggling writers; it also occasionally led to his convincing himself that some famous author was "poverty-stricken" when in fact he was flourishing.

Every evening after dinner at the Villa Mauresque, in the days before the war, Annette, his famous cook, would come in with the menu book and stand behind his chair, and Willie would put on his spectacles to order the meals for the following day. This would be the moment when all of us staying at the villa would know who was coming to lunch the next day. If a successful author was coming, Willie would take this opportunity to begin his ploy of making us believe that the man was penniless.

I took notes each time that this happened, so I am able to reproduce a specific occasion.

As Annette stood behind his chair Willie removed his spectacles and looked up at us mourfully, "Noël is coming to lunch tomorrow," he announced.

We all murmured approval. We all knew Noël Coward; we all liked him.

"Poor Noël,' Willie said sadly, "I suppose you know that he's right down on his uppers?"

44

"Down on his uppers!" someone exclaimed in astonishment. "I thought he was rolling in money."

"He *was*," Willie said, "but it's all gone. Every penny of it. His plays don't go as well as they used to. The last two were a flop. His backers lost their shirts. And I'm told that all poor Noël's investments have gone down the drain. He hasn't got a cent left."

We were all left speechless by this information.

"He won't have had a square meal for weeks," Willie continued. "So we'd better give him something substantial."

Willie turned to Annette.

"*Alors, pour commencer on prendrait une soupe à l'oignon*," he said. "*Et ensuite un steak-et-kidney pudding. Et pour terminer un soufflé au chocolat.*"

"*Bien, monsieur,*" said Annette. "*Bonsoir, monsieur.*"

"*Bonsoir, Annette,*" said Willie, and turned once again to us.

"You know, when people are down on their luck they're apt to get rather touchy," he said. "So I must ask you to be here waiting for him at a quarter to one tomorrow when Noël arrives. I don't want him to feel ser-slighted."

By this time Willie had managed to convince even the most doubtful of us that Noël wasn't quite as successful as we had supposed. So punctually at a quarter to one on that hot summer day we were assembled waiting to greet the famous (but apparently now down-at-heel) writer. Punctually Noël Coward arrived. He looked very well-fed and extremely affluent, and indeed we were subsequently to discover that he was both.

"Willie," he cried. "*Cher maître!*" And he embraced him warmly. Willie gently detached himself.

"I'm sure you need a cocktail," Willie said with a meaning look towards us.

"I'd love one," Noël said, sprightly as ever.

Noël was given his first cocktail. By the time the shaker had been handed round the room, Noël, who was rather disconcerted by our surreptitious glances towards his shoes, had finished his glass.

"Noël would like *another* cocktail," Willie said.

Noël's glass was refilled.

"*Monsieur est servi*," the butler announced.

In we went to lunch—with Noël still sparkling gaily but perhaps slightly nervously. By the time he had finished the steaming bowl of onion soup, beads of sweat stood out on Noël's forehead and the bright torrent of his conversation had been reduced to a trickle. When the steak-and-kidney pudding was brought in, he raised his eyes in silent anguish to the ceiling.

"*Servez bien Monsieur Coward*," said Willie. "*Il a l'air d'avoir faim*. He looks quite famished."

Noël stared down in dismay at the vast helping on his plate. But Noël was always polite and splendidly gallant, and he finished every bit of it. Then, round came the chocolate soufflé sizzling in the torrid Riviera heat, and Noël's eyes once again rolled plaintively to the ceiling. But once more he got through it manfully, though his shirt was now drenched with sweat.

After coffee and liqueurs I escorted Noël to his car. He was exhausted by sheer weight of food. It was with an effort that he spoke at all.

"Wonderful old boy," Noël said. "But a trifle over-hospitable, don't you think?"

"I suppose you noticed how quickly he drank his first two cocktails," Willie was saying when I came back into the house. "He obviously needed a decent drink. And did you see how he wolfed down the steak-and-kidney pudding? *And* the chocolate soufflé? He probably hadn't had a square meal for weeks."*

*   *   *

A few days later when Barbara and I were again lying by the pool, she began telling me about Gerald.

"You know, he not only drinks far too heavily—and I don't say that because I am totally teetotal myself—but he's also a reckless gambler," she told me. "Willie was having a cure in France, to get thin. Gerald was taking me to Paris. Gerald decided we would be passing the cure place if we went about eighty miles out of our way and we could see Willie, which would please him. So we did, and Willie *was* very pleased to see us. Except Gerald lost £100 at the casino; though I didn't hear of this until later. Gerald had a flat in Paris, and when we got there we went out to dinner. Gerald was rather tight and in a terrible state of nerves.

"I asked him what was the matter, and he said, 'I'm terribly in debt.'

"In fact it turned out that he was something like £3,000 in debt.

" 'I dare not tell Willie,' he said.

"I told him that I would tell Willie.

" 'Do you dare?' he asked.

" 'Yes, I'll do it,' I said.

"So next day I went back to England. Willie came to London after his cure, and Gerald went to the Mauresque. I asked if I could see Willie alone. I was very nervous of

---

* I used this story of Noël's visit to the Mauresque in my book *Somerset and All the Maughams* (Longmans and Heinemann, London, 1966). But since Noël was still alive and I thought that even a hint that his talent had once looked as if it was failing would offend him, I changed the name of the guest to Vivian Parry.

the whole thing. But Willie took it beautifully. 'I shall pay Gerald's debts and I will deduct it from his wages,' he said. Willie is not very generous to Gerald with wages, you know—but Gerald takes what he wants, as I'm sure you know. Willie told me later that Gerald never told the truth about his debts; he always left off the odd £500.

"Gerald is generous. He would give you £100. But he also expects others to be generous with him," Barbara told me.

"One evening Gerald and Willie and I went to Monte Carlo to a gala of some sort. Afterwards Willie was tired and went home. Gerald, slightly tight, immediately went to the gambling room with me. 'Sit by me, Babs,' he said, 'you bring me luck.' It's strange, Gerald is the only person who has ever called me Babs.

"I don't gamble, so I don't know much about it. But at the beginning Gerald won, and every time I saw a big plaque in his winnings I picked it up quietly and put it in my bag. He was too tight to notice. Eventually my bag was full of plaques. Then Gerald's luck changed. He cashed another cheque at the *caisse* and he lost. He became very angry and used very bad language to me.

"There were some English people there and they were embarrassed. So I went with them to a café over the road. Ten minutes later Gerald arrived. He was very depressed. He had lost his money, and he had violent hiccoughs. This made me giggle, and of course that made him worse. I was over my rage by now, and we got into the car with Jean the chauffeur, and we drove back from Monte Carlo to the Mauresque, Gerald still hiccoughing madly.

" 'I'm in an awful mess,' Gerald told me. 'I don't know *how* much I lost. There will be a frightful row with Willie.'

48

"So I opened my purse and poured the plaques out on to the floor of the car. 'I don't understand this money,' I said. 'But there's enough to pay for what you lost.'

" 'My darling Babsie-boo!' Gerald cried. 'You've saved my life.'

"We got down on the floor of the car to count it up. I said, 'Now, Gerald, pay what you owe and you'll be all right.'

" 'You're an angel!' Gerald exclaimed.

"When we arrived back at the Mauresque, Gerald walked with me to my room and left me at the door. As you are aware, no one ever calls you at the Mauresque. You ring the bell when you awaken. So in the morning, I rang for the maid and she came in with my breakfast. 'Mr Maugham is very anxious to see you,' she said. 'Please bring him in,' I replied.

"Willie came in, wearing his usual Chinese dressing-gown with slits at the sides. 'Where is Gerald?' he asked.

" 'In bed,' I told him.

" 'He's not in bed,' Willie said. 'He hasn't been to bed; his bed has not been slept in.'

" 'Well, he left me outside my bedroom at five a.m.,' I said. 'I presumed that he was going to bed. What shall we do—call the police?' We were both worried. It seemed that he had told Jean to go to bed and had taken the car on himself. We were afraid that he had crashed the car because he's such a mad driver. Anyway, we didn't call the police. We spent the morning in the garden; we swam in the pool. We had a sad lunch; we had said all we could say. Then the butler came in. 'Would you come outside, sir?' he said to Willie.

"Willie got up and we both went outside.

"At the front door, there in the large sweep of drive, *there* we saw Jean in the big car. And by the side of him

49

there was Gerald, sitting in a little new two-seater car, as tight as a tick, holding a large bottle of scent in his hand.

" 'This is for you, Barbara,' he announced. 'And Willie —I've bought you a car.'

"Gerald had returned to the casino and had doubled the money I had given him and bought our presents with his winnings.

"This shows another side of Gerald," Barbara said. "Willie used that car for ages."

*   *   *

On one of our walks Willie suddenly turned to me and said, "You know, I'm per-perfectly aware that Gerald is both a drunkard and a gambler. I don't think of him as an angel, but he does have great qualities."

*   *   *

At my next "session" with Barbara by the pool, she told me a little more about Willie's relationship with Gerald.

"Over the years Gerald has almost always been full of charm and full of liquor—in almost equal parts," she said. "But if Willie is invited to a party, he always makes sure that Gerald is invited with him. The trouble is that Gerald feels himself snubbed or ignored. One evening, several years ago, we were all invited to an enormous party given by some retired film star and his wife. Almost as soon as we arrived there, Gerald disappeared to a bar which had been set up at the far end of the garden. Presently he approached the group of people in which Willie was standing. Gerald was swaying slightly.

" 'I don't know about you, ducky,' he said to Willie, 'but I'm going down to the pool to have a swim.'

"At the word 'ducky' Willie stiffened. There was silence, then a titter. Willie did not move. Gerald lurched away. A few moments later our hostess appeared and came up to Willie. 'I'm sorry we can't swim tonight,' she said, 'but the pool's been emptied.'

"Willie stared at her for a second in silence, then made some excuse and moved swiftly away. When he was out of sight he began to run towards the pool which was in a part of the garden not floodlit that evening. At the bottom of the empty pool, Gerald was lying crumpled and motionless, naked except for his white briefs. Blood was seeping from his head. He was in hospital for several months."

But I knew that Willie always forgave Gerald's transgressions, for in many ways he was a wonderful companion for him. Willie was shy and reticent; he was frequently depressed and silent. Gerald, an excellent host unless drunk, was ebulliently, irrepressibly friendly.

When the two men travelled around the world together, it was Gerald who made the contacts that Willie needed for his stories. Gerald helped him find the raw material he wanted for his work; his boisterous spirits could lift him from his occasional fits of gloom. Gerald's diligence saved Willie from all the minor irritations of travel, and his resourcefulness, at least on one occasion when they were out sailing in Borneo, saved Willie's life; for had Gerald lost his head when—in Willie's words—the 'great mass of water . . . caught the boat and turned it over', my uncle would have been drowned. As it was, this incident almost cost Gerald *his* life—for as soon as he had managed to get Willie to the river bank, Gerald had a heart attack. This incident later formed the basis for Willie's short story "The Yellow Streak".

* * *

I believe that one of the reasons Gerald still drank so much, even after his accident at the swimming-pool, was because he was sometimes bored with the life he had to lead.

At my next visit to the Mauresque, Willie, Gerald and I went one evening to Villefranche where we had dinner on the small terrace of a restaurant which overlooked the yachts moored in the harbour. Gerald was already getting drunk. He kept calling for more cognacs and this was slightly irritating Willie. "Why do you always have to drink so much?" Willie asked.

"I might as well ask why you drink so little," Gerald replied.

"For two reasons," Willie answered. "The first is that I've been endowed with a certain force of character. And the second—as you know perfectly well—is that if I have one drink too many I'm as sick as a dog . . . But I repeat, why do *you* always have to drink so much?"

Gerald said, "Because it makes life look rosier," and he turned towards me, "Don't you agree, Robin?"

"I must confess, I do," I answered.

Willie ignored my interruption. He never took his eyes off Gerald. "Isn't your life a whole bed of roses?" he asked. "I would have thought it was."

With a sudden nervous flick of his wrist, Gerald flung away the cigarette he had been smoking.

"What's wrong?" Willie asked gently.

"I'm getting bored," Gerald said, "that's what's wrong."

"We go to enough parties in all conscience," Willie said.

"I only get asked because of you," Gerald told him. "I'm just a nonentity who happens to be your friend . . .

People only invite me because they know that if they don't, you won't come."

"Gerald, that's untrue," Willie protested. "Half the people we know find you vastly more entertaining than they do me."

"I've got my own friends, and I like parties with them," Gerald admitted. "But at that kind of party you can't join in. You're always aloof and observing. You can't enjoy life as anyone else does. You even bricked up the window of your writing-room to shut out the view."

"You know it distracted me from my work," Willie said.

"That's just like you," Gerald told him. "Nothing matters but your work."

Gerald paused and beckoned to the waiter for further cognac. Willie sighed.

"Even when I'm alone with you," Gerald continued, "somehow I don't feel you're there. It's a stranger who's watching me. I feel that you're registering everything I do, everything I say, so that you can make me a character in one of your books. You can't give of yourself to anyone —can you?"

"I happen to believe in making the best of my deficiencies," Willie told him.

"Your work is all you really care for," Gerald said. "You've given up everything for that, haven't you? Love, peace, leisure, happiness. You've sold the lot for it, haven't you? I can see it now . . ."

"Oh, my dear Gerald . . ." Willie murmured.

"No, ducky. I'm right, and you know it. The most I could ever hope for was second place. I suppose it's fun while it lasts. But your work comes first. You're dedicated. You don't even own your own soul . . . But I wonder just who does."

53

Suddenly Willie's face grew taut. He spoke coldly. "Gerald, you've had too much to drink," he said. "It's time we went home." Then Willie's face softened. "Don't forget—you'll be having a late night tomorrow. Remember, we have plans for young Robin." Willie turned towards me. "Gerald and I have decided that all your talk of romantic love is balls," he said. "What you really need is a good romp. So tomorrow night Gerald has gallantly volunteered to drive you into Nice and take you to a bordello or two. You'll soon find out what you want."

The next evening Jean drove Gerald and me along the Corniche to Nice. First Gerald took me to various *louche* bars which he often frequented. Then, when we were both slightly drunk, we began to make our tour of the brothels. The routine was always the same. Gerald would greet the madame who ran the bordello and order a bottle of champagne. Presently, the girls would parade naked before us. And I was appalled.

My conscience was revolted by the spectacle of such degradation. Yet I could not help noticing that the girls seemed perfectly happy and indifferent to whether they were chosen or not. It was this brazen indifference which, I found, reduced completely such ardour as might have arisen in me. I could not see myself having any of them and, soon after midnight, I begged Gerald to give up the quest. But Gerald was drunkenly determined to find a girl who would please me—and he did. In the next brothel we visited I saw that one of the girls looked shy and embarrassed. She was about my age, wonderfully slim and attractive. Without hesitation I chose her. She led me up a flight of rickety stairs to her bedroom. While I undressed she told me that she was a stenographer in

54

Paris. But in order to pay for her holiday in Nice she worked in the brothel twice a week.

*   *   *

After tea the following day, I went for a walk with Willie. "Did you enjoy yourself last night?" he asked me.

"Enormously," I said.

"I'm glad," Willie said. "That proves my per-point. All you needed was a good romp without all this silly romantic fiddle-faddle. But of course that kind of pleasure costs money. As I've told you before now, money is the sixth sense which enables us to enjoy the other five. For some reason that escapes me, people seem to regret that money costs money. They refuse to recognise its importance. My brother Harry was always poor and it embittered his whole life. He wrote dreadful plays in blank verse which were praised by various high-brow critics but which never made him a cent.

"After my first novel—*Liza of Lambeth*—had had quite a success and was completely sold out, I told Harry that I'd decided to chuck medicine and follow his example by taking up writing as a career. He was appalled. 'Your little novel has had a *succès de scandale* —but no more,' he told me. 'You can make a decent living as a doctor; why not stick to it?' If I'd taken his advice my whole life would have been different. He was quite emphatic about it. 'None of the important critics have taken you seriously,' he told me. 'After all, you must realise that my *Life of Saint Francis of Assisi* was reviewed by every serious journal in the country. But you haven't even got a foot on the ladder.'

"I didn't like to tell him that one could starve in a garret for all the good the intellectual reviewers could do one. I knew even then—as I now know—that it's the

55

public that counts, not the critics. And of course poor Harry couldn't abide it—and even though those early books of mine were hardly a howling success, at least they were being published and making me some money. At that time I'd had only one play performed and published, though I had written others. Harry told me that my plays, like my novels, were well constructed and neatly contrived but they were also trivial and shallow because the life I was leading was trivial and shallow. He had come around to ask me to have supper with him. But I couldn't go with him as I already had a date. When I explained that I had a prior engagement, Harry's reaction was bitterly sarcastic. He looked through the open door which led to my bedroom; he could see my evening clothes laid out on the cover of the bed. 'Some smart dinner party, I suppose?' he said. 'Precisely,' I answered, 'but I don't see why you should disapprove.' 'Because you are living in a world to which you don't belong,' Harry told me. 'What world *do* I belong to?' I asked him. 'The world of reality,' he answered, 'the world of a young Cockney girl in the slums of Lambeth—or perhaps the world of a little newspaper boy trudging up the streets of Whitstable.' 'Why do you keep referring to that newspaper boy?' I asked him. 'Why do you keep dragging him into our conversations together?' 'Because—since our mother died—he's the only person you've ever been able to love,' Harry told me. 'You call a boyhood friendship love?' I asked. 'Yes, I do,' he said. 'Aren't you perhaps endowing me with your own tastes?' I asked. 'Perhaps,' he answered, 'only time can show. Perhaps one day you can find a girl with whom you can fall in love—and if that happens, make sure of your own nature before it happens and you take that final step.' 'And how on earth can I do that?' I asked him.

"It's odd how clearly I can recall the words he spoke as he stood there in his shabby suit. 'You just walk along any street quite slowly,' he told me, 'and notice which way your eyes wander.' I was irritated. 'Sometimes your advice is as obscure as the plots of the plays you write,' I told him. 'You know just what I mean,' he replied. 'As for the present, believe me, this raffish Bohemian set you're in with is like an octopus. It will suck the life-blood from you, mark my words.'

"I was now angry. 'I do mark your words, Harry,' I told him. 'But I mark them three out of ten—because I have a notion that they are dictated either from ignorance or from envy. And I have a notion that you don't have to dine in Mayfair to be trivial and shallow. I am sure you can be equally trivial and shallow in the gutter.' "

Willie was silent for a moment. I looked at him. His face was grim. "I shall never forgive myself for those words," he told me. "You see the effect on Harry was disastrous. He flinched as if I'd struck him. 'I might have known it would only be a matter of time before you'd fling my poverty in my face,' he told me. He moved towards the door. I tried to stop him. 'I didn't mean it,' I said, 'you mustn't be so over-sensitive.' But it was too late. He had already left the room. I would have run after him, but I was already late for dinner. So I dressed quickly and went out to my dinner party.

"A few nights later, when I came back from some party or other, I was surprised to find my landlady sitting on a chair in the hall. She seemed to be rather distressed. She got up quickly as I came in. I had a terrible premonition. 'What's wrong?' I asked. 'It's your brother, Harry,' she told me. 'His landlady heard a crash as if he'd had a bad fall. She went rushing upstairs but the door was locked.

57

She and her husband could hear Harry groaning . . . so they broke in. It's terrible. He's taken poison. They didn't like to send for a doctor because they're afraid he'd send for the police.' I rushed out and got a cab. Harry lived in a lodging house in Cadogan Street. His landlady opened the door for me. 'Thank God you've come,' she said. I ran up the stairs.

"Harry was lying fully dressed on a high brass bedstead in a corner of the shabbily furnished bedroom. He was gasping and writhing with pain. On the table by the bed was a bottle of nitric acid. What made everything more unbearable was that he'd made a terrible botch of it. He hadn't taken enough acid and had been in agony ever since. I managed to get him into my cab and took him to St Thomas's Hospital where I'd been a student. They did all they could . . . Ber-but it was too late. He died shortly afterwards.

"Poor Harry, he was misguided. But at least there was more warmth and milk of human kindess about him than there is about your sainted father. *He* disapproves not only of my wealth but also of my whole way of life. Your father feels that to ignore the laws of the Almighty deserves nothing less than death. He likes mixing with what he calls 'clean, decent people'. With your mother it's different. In her heart of hearts she may disapprove of my way of life but there's always been an affection between us. Your mother is a devout Christian, but she's tolerant of my foibles. She was of course quite shocked by *Liza of Lambeth* and one or two of my later books. But she's always got over it. I'm very fond of your mother—even though she's the kind of woman who likes to eat cold mutton in a howling draught. But she has generosity of heart and a wonderful vitality."

* * *

During my subsequent visits to the Mauresque, though Willie was always kind to me, I felt that I could see a slight change in him. Sometimes when I was in the long living-room that overlooked the lovely patio with its orange trees, Willie would be unaware that I was in the room. I would look at him. I suppose he was thinking about his characters, but from the grim look on his face I felt that something was haunting Willie—something evil. And I felt that it was something in the future rather than the present—because although Gerald could be described as "wicked" in many ways, he was certainly not evil. Why therefore was Willie haunted? Willie had accused me of being a romantic and not a realist. But I could not help myself from wondering if Gerald's drunken meanderings in Vienna about Aleister Crowley did possess some odd element of truth. For sometimes in the living-room when Willie was alone, I would gaze at a man in his middle sixties whose face betrayed no physical suffering. His face held the expression of a person who was haunted.

But on board Gerald's yacht, the *Sara*, a forty-five ton converted fishing-boat, Willie seemed to be at peace. He would sit on deck, smoking a cigarette and gazing out at the clear blue water around us. Sometimes his glance would flicker over the body of the slim cabin boy whom Gerald had picked up in a bar in Paris.

"Let's leave together on a long cruise," Gerald suggested one afternoon. "Let's spend a whole year around the Greek islands."

"We der-daren't make a cruise yet awhile," Willie told him.

"Why not?" Gerald asked.

"Haven't you been reading the papers?" Willie asked.

"The wretched Hitler has got his eyes on the whole of Europe and there are rumours of war."

"To hell with Hitler," Gerald said. "Don't let's worry. We got through the war the last time and somehow we'll do it if there's another."

"There mustn't be another," Willie said.

"I dare say," Gerald replied. "But what can you do to stop it?"

"In my own little way I did try to stop it. Gerald, you typed out *For Services Rendered*. Can you remember the words?"

"I can," Gerald answered.

Willie turned to me. "Your sainted father told me he'd found the play most unpatriotic. But at least you seemed to have liked it."

"I certainly did," I answered.

Willie paused for a moment. "I don't think I shall ever forget Cedric Hardwicke in the role of Sydney. Do you remember the speech? I can remember every word." Willie began to quote from his anti-war play—which had been misunderstood by audiences and critics when first staged in 1932; *For Services Rendered* was not the kind of play audiences expected from the author of such plays as *The Circle* and *Our Betters*, and it failed. "I know that we were the dupes of the incompetent fools who ruled the nations," Willie's speech began. "I know that we were sacrificed to their vanity, their greed and their stupidity. And the worst of it is that as far as I can tell they haven't learnt a thing. They're just as vain, they're just as stupid as they ever were."

Willie paused for a moment. I was conscious that as he had been speaking these lines from his play—as on the occasions when he spoke in public—his stammer seemed completely to disappear. Willie lit a cigarette, but it slowly burned down in his fingers as he continued to speak the words from his play. "They muddle on, muddle on, and one of these days they'll muddle us all into another war," Willie quoted, and suddenly looked directly at Gerald and me. Then he continued to speak. "When that happens I'll tell you what I'm going to do. I'm going out into the streets and cry: 'Look at me; don't be a lot of damned fools; it's all bunk what they're saying to you, about honour and patriotism and glory, bunk, bunk, bunk.' " Willie paused for a moment; he tossed the butt of his cigarette over the side of the yacht. "At the first night the audience sat in complete silence at the end of that speech. I think it shocked them in a way. But I knew that I'd failed. I knew it was no use because they would never understand."

For a moment the three of us sat in silence. Then Gerald spoke, "You were just another voice crying in the wilderness," he said. "They didn't listen to you, ducky, any more than they listen to your friend Churchill." Then Gerald paused. The atmosphere seemed to have become suddenly gloomy. Gerald stood up. "Now I propose to make us a delicious cocktail," he said.

*　　*　　*

The following morning I found Willie sitting in a deep wicker armchair with canvas-covered cushions set by a marble-topped table placed between the orange trees on the terrace overlooking the vast garden and the bay beyond. Gerald was standing by the drink trolley pouring out a Daiquiri.

"You know what's happening this afternoon, Robin?" Gerald asked me.

"What?" I asked.

"Your illustrious uncle . . ." Gerald began.

"Your illustrious *aged* uncle," Willie corrected him.

"Your illustrious and aged uncle," Gerald continued, "all of sixty-five—is being invested by the Mayor of Nice with the Order of the Légion d'Honneur for his services to literature and to France."

"Can I come and watch?" I asked.

"Yes," Willie replied. "But you must promise not to giggle. To them it will be an important and solemn occasion."

Gerald handed Willie his drink. "Thank you, my dear Gerald," Willie said. "That's most kind of you." Willie sipped his drink thoughtfully. "You know, Robin," he said, "I've lived here over ten years now and I love France... It is more home to me than ever England could be. I only wish that I weren't so utterly convinced that politically the country is so completely rotten and corrupt... and I wish to heavens that our incompetent politicians in England didn't have so much confidence in her as an ally."

Gerald finished his Daiquiri and began to mix another. "But now that your brother Freddie has become Lord Chancellor of England," he said, "he's one of those politicians you're talking about. He's in the Cabinet. Why not go and see him?"

Willie turned to me. "Do you think your sainted father would deign to listen to me?" he asked.

"Yes," I said. "He'd *listen* all right!"

"Perhaps I'll write to him first," Willie murmured. "You could take the letter back with you."

*   *   *

I met Willie in London at the Garrick Club a week or so later. He had seen my father in the House of Lords that afternoon.

62

"It was all very impressive," Willie told me. "I was ushered into an imposing room overlooking the Thames. Presently Freddie, wearing his robes and a long-bottomed wig, came into the room. He took off his wig and placed it on a wig stand. Then he removed his robes. 'I read your long letter with interest,' he told me.

" 'I've since had proof that at least one member of the French Cabinet is in the pay of Germany,' I informed him.

" 'We've heard similar rumours over here,' your father replied. 'But on examination they have proved to be false.'

" 'But I've seen a photograph of a cheque paid to the man's wife,' I told him.

"That didn't convince your father at all. 'Probably a forgery put about by some other politician to discredit his rival,' he informed me.

"I decided I must be more direct. 'You don't believe me when I tell you that politically France is corrupt?' I asked.

" 'I take it with a pinch of salt,' he replied.

" 'If there's war,' I said, 'France will cave in like a rotten apple.'

" 'My dear Willie,' your father said in his most patronising voice, 'you must allow me to know better. I am not one of the incompetent fools who rule England that you write so sneeringly about . . . As a member of the Cabinet you will appreciate that the most secret Intelligence documents are sent to me. You are not even a politician, you are a novelist out of touch with reality. I therefore have every reason to disbelieve almost everything you've said—both in your letter and in conversation this afternoon. And in any case—you can take it from me—there will be no war.'

"Your father was so definite that I realised there wasn't anything more I could say."

*   *   *

When the war broke out, the British government asked Willie to write morale-boosting propaganda stories about the state of France. Willie reluctantly agreed to write these stories—but he found the going very heavy. When it was obvious that France was going to fall, Willie decided to return to England in search of war work: 'I should have liked to find something to do in England,' Willie wrote to me, 'and the Ministry of Information have written to tell me that they may be able to use my services, but I realise that with the whole country eager to get some occupation connected with the war, they could find as many people as they want younger and perhaps more competent than I; so I much fear that I shall be left to twiddle my thumbs indefinitely.'

Willie returned to England on an over-crowded collier—the voyage to England took three weeks; each passenger was rationed to one pint of water each day for drinking and washing purposes. As the United States was not yet in the war Gerald, with his American passport, stayed on at the Mauresque—packing up Willie's valuable collection of pictures and bibelots. It was mainly due to Gerald's diligence that virtually all of Willie's treasures survived the war unharmed. Willie left France in July 1940, from Marseilles. On his arrival in London I got leave from my regiment, which was soon to go to the Western Desert, in order to dine with him at the Savoy. That evening he talked about his journey from Marseilles to London.

"Der-do you know that the most amazing thing happened to me on board the boat," Willie told me. "The

64

captain of the ship came up to me and said he wanted to see me in his cabin. Naturally, I wondered what it was all about. At my advanced age I didn't think he'd taken a fancy to me. But I will confess that I was surprised by what he said after he'd given me a whisky and soda. 'Mr Maugham,' he began, 'I'm addressing you not as the captain of this ship, but as a deputy for the passengers.'

" 'Yes?' I replied, wondering what in heaven's name he was going to say.

" 'As you know,' he continued, 'with this strict black-out we are forced to have, the nights seem very long.' He gave a short laugh. 'Particularly when a torpedo from a submarine may blow us up at any moment. Not that I give your fellow passengers *that* piece of information,' he added. 'But for all of them, the long evenings are a bit of a strain.'

" 'Precisely,' I agreed. 'But what can I do to help?'

" 'To come to the point,' the captain continued, 'some of the passengers thought it might make the time pass by more quickly if you told them a few stories.'

" 'But I couldn't do that!' I exclaimed.

" 'Why not?' the captain asked.

" 'I wouldn't know where to begin,' I told him.

"The captain smiled at me. 'If I may say so, Mr Maugham,' he said, 'you've been writing to my certain knowledge for forty years, so surely by now you can tell a story!'

Willie took a sip of his wine. "Under the circumstances I could hardly refuse," he continued. "But I cer-can't tell you what a strange experience it was to sit on that open deck surrounded by passengers sprawling all around me, with the stars clear in the sky above. Each time I'd pause for a moment in the tale I was telling them, we could

65

hear the throb of the ship's engine and the wash of the waves."

"What stories *did* you tell them?" I asked.

"Any that came into my head," Willie answered. "And the strange thing was that though the passengers were an odd mixture—retired colonels and their ladies, oily-faced stokers, women of fashion and schoolgirls—they were a far better audience than any I've ever addressed when giving lectures. They listened intently to every word I said. Amongst the stories I told was one I heard when I was in Fiji.

"There were two Englishmen—two copra merchants —who shared a bungalow. They were close friends, and they'd always got on well together. Now, they'd always wanted a dog. And one day a mutual friend gave them a young Labrador. And at first they were both delighted."

Willie paused for a moment and lit a cigarette.

"They both became devoted to the dog," Willie continued. "And each of them wanted the dog to like *him* the best. Each wanted the dog to sit beside him or to sleep curled up at his feet. And gradually their relationship became strained. The two of them had been friends for twenty years, but now they began to bicker and quarrel. Each of them resented it—when the dog would make a fuss of the other. Their jealousy over the dog was ruining their friendship that had lasted over so many long years . . ."

Willie stubbed out his cigarette.

"Finally, on a hot sultry evening—when the air was so close you could hardly breathe," Willie continued, "one of the two friends—the older one—went into the hall and picked up a gun." Willie began to speak more slowly and deliberately as he reached the climax of his story. "Then

66

he called the dog to him . . . And he led the dog outside the compound . . . And he shot it dead."

*   *   *

"I felt like the story-teller from the thousand and one nights," Willie said. "But if that ghastly journey had lasted any longer I'd have run out of stories."

"What will you do now?" I asked.

"I've tried to get work in Intelligence again. But they say I'm too old—I'm sixty-six, you know. And even your sainted father can't help me find a job. So I shall go to the States—I agreed to meet Gerald in New York, anyway—and move down to South Carolina where my American publisher has found me a little house. I'm afraid Gerald will get very bored and will probably drink too much. And the doctors say that if he goes on drinking it will kill him eventually. But I hope that the quiet of South Carolina will help him to relax." Willie smiled at me. "But what about you? I hear your regiment's going overseas," he said. "Have you any idea where? Or is it top security?"

"Well, since we've been issued with Arctic clothes," I told him, "the betting's ten to one on the Middle East."

Willie raised his glass to me. "Well, my dear," he said, "I drink to you. And, incidentally, I hope you realise what an important man you're dining with. I have been personally denounced by Herr Goebbels."

67

Part Two

In December 1941, Willie moved to South Carolina where Nelson Doubleday, his American publisher, had built a comfortable eight-room house, called Parker's Ferry, on his plantation twelve miles from Yemassee, in desolate yet oddly beautiful country. Parker's Ferry had a lovely view over a huge marsh in front and a wood of pine trees behind; it was two miles from the nearest house, twenty-four miles from the nearest small town—to which Willie went for provisions—and more than fifty miles from the nearest large town, Charleston. Willie enjoyed the peace and simplicity of his life there; he liked the placid routine. But the place was far too quiet for Gerald, who soon became restive. He was only just fifty; he was bright and virile, and he felt the war was a challenge to him to prove himself in his own right. He had grown tired of being tolerated by Willie's friends as a useful adjunct to Willie's existence. He wanted to succeed—personally and publicly —on his own, so he took a clerical war job. With Gerald in Washington, Willie spent much of his time alone— though he had two black maids to look after him who thought him the funniest man they had ever met. In 1943, Willie wrote to me from New York—he had just finished *The Razor's Edge* and was presumably there in connection with the publication—"Gerald is working very hard providing food for three thousand people and liking the job. It is a marvel to see him getting up at six-thirty to go to work and getting home just before eight." Gerald was staying with Willie at that moment, but he was looking for a small house at Garden City where he could settle down. Gerald was happier than he had been in years, Willie wrote, and he appeared to be giving his employers great satisfaction. The letter concluded with the words: "So everything is fine."

But everything wasn't so fine. In Washington, divorced from Willie's care and sobering influence, Gerald literally worked and drank himself to death. On June 26th, 1944, Willie wrote to me to say that Gerald was very ill. He had had an attack of pleurisy in Washington and had then developed tuberculosis of the lungs. He looked pitifully wasted. Willie was taking him to a sanatorium in the Adironacks, where the fine air might save him. Gerald, Willie wrote, had been very good, patient and cheerful, but he had not been told how dangerously ill he was. There was only a small chance of saving him and, if he did survive, Gerald would have to lead the life of a semi-invalid for as long as he lived.

In November 1944, Gerald died in Doctors' Hospital in New York. Willie, stricken with grief, travelled down to South Carolina, buried himself in his remote little house in the wilds of Yemassee, and went—I can think of no other phrase to describe his condition—into a decline. He refused to leave Parker's Ferry and he refused to meet anyone—even his closest friends. It was then that Ellen and Nelson Doubleday suggested that I should come out to stay with him. I was ill and jittery as a result of a head wound received in the Western Desert. The calm of Yemassee might restore my nerves; my presence might help to drag Willie from his decline. I was keen to go. And thanks to the kindness of Brendan Bracken in the Ministry of Information and Victor Weybright, his

American opposite number in London, I managed to get a passage on a ship to Halifax, Nova Scotia. When I arrived at Yemassee, I found Willie overwhelmed with misery.

"With the pills they've given me, I sometimes manage to sleep or doze for as much as six hours a night," he told me. "But I think of Gerald every single minute that I'm awake. I try to forget him all the eighteen hours of the day. You can't imagine what it was like—hour after hour —listening to that terrible cough that seemed to tear him to pieces."

Suddenly Willie lowered himself on to the sofa and buried his face in his hands. He began to cry with long racking sobs. "You'll never know how great this grief has been to me," he said when he had controlled himself and could speak again. "The best years of my life—those we spent wandering about the world—are inextricably connected with him. And in one way or another—however indirectly—all I've written during the last twenty years has something to do with him, if only that he typed my manuscripts for me." Suddenly Willie was again shaken with sobs. "I try to forget," he moaned, "but a dozen times a day something I come across, something I read, a stray word reminds me of him and I am overcome with grief." Willie became a little calmer. "They tell me time will help, but time flows dreadfully slowly. For thirty years he had been my chief care, my pleasure and my anxiety. Without him I am lost and lonely and hopeless. He was nearly twenty years younger than I was, and I had every right to think that he would have survived me. He would have been terribly upset at my death, but he would have got drunk for a week or two and then reconciled himself to it, for he had a naturally happy

73

temper, but I am too old to endure so much grief. I have lived too long."

Willie seemed inconsolable. But at least my arrival forced him to make a slight effort to recover. He took me to dine with Ellen and Nelson Doubleday and their family in what we both called "the big house", and their friendliness and splendid if erratic hospitality did much to restore both of us. As the sunlit days passed by, Willie began to look less forlorn, and soon he began to manage a shaky smile. But it was not until New Year's Eve that I realised that Willie had managed to steer himself round the corner towards recovery.

There was a large party up at the big house on New Year's Eve. Willie and I were invited. A minute or so before midnight someone gaily suggested that we should all sing "Auld Lang Syne". Immediately Willie's face froze with dismay—not because he was afraid that the hackneyed tune would remind him of Gerald: by now he could cope with that misery. I could see from his hectic glances to right and to left that the reason for his consternation was more superficial and immediate. From childhood Willie had had a morbid dread of physical contact with strangers, and he was now suddenly confronted with the prospect of his hands being crossed and then clasped in the sticky palms of two unknown females who had come in late and who were now standing on either side of him. Into his eyes came the look of a frantic hunted animal. I was wondering how Willie would get out of his predicament, when he spoke:

"When on New Year's Eve," Willie said, "I hear people singing that song in which they ask themselves the question 'should old acquaintance be forgot?' I can only ter-tell you that my own answer is in the affirmative."

That did the trick. Hands that had been crossed and

74

outstretched to clasp Willie's fell down in limp despondency. Mouths that had been open to chant merrily closed with a snap. And Willie had saved himself. At that instant he caught me looking at him and gave me a broad wink, and I knew that for a while at least he was back to his old form again.

Later that night, when we had returned to Willie's little house, we sat before the dying embers of the fire, having one last drink before going to bed. We had been sitting in silence for some moments, sipping our drinks, enjoying our cigarettes. Then Willie spoke:

"Gerald always insisted on us having a nightcap before we went to bed..." he said. "You know, if I believed in God, I'd pray that I could join him soon. But I'm nearly seventy, so I haven't long to wait... As Epicurus said— there's nothing terrible in not living... I'm a millionaire, and they tell me that I'm the most famous writer alive. But I don't really care... I shall go back to the Mauresque eventually. I suppose I might as well live there as anywhere..."

*   *   *

Though Willie seemed to be getting back to his old form again, I wasn't. I was very nervous, and I couldn't rid myself of my own stammer, which had begun after my head wound. At times I felt suicidally depressed as I thought of the friends in my regiment, officers and men, who had been killed or maimed in the desert. I thought of my nephew David, who had been severely wounded three times, and of his brother John, who had been killed in Germany. In the wilds of Yemassee I came to the conclusion that I was close to going mad. One day I asked Willie if he thought that a psychiatrist could help my condition.

75

"No," said Willie firmly. "Certainly not."

"Why not?"

"Because he could do you no good. Your injury has exaggerated your defects, that's all. And you can't change your essential nature. All you can try to do is make the best of your limitations."

Willie looked at my doubtful face. "I can ser-see you don't believe a word I'm saying. I can see that you think I'm being wilfully obtuse," he said. "So I'll tell you a story to show my point."

Willie wandered over to the side-table and began to mix a dry martini. "Years ago," he said, "long before the First World War, I was quite fer-famous because I had four plays running in London at the same time, and I came to New York for the rehearsals of one of them. I was staying at the Ritz-Carlton, I remember. And one afternoon they rang up from the desk to say that there was a Mr Maugham waiting downstairs to see me.

" 'There's a mistake,' I told them. 'I'm Mr Maugham.'

" 'We know,' the desk clerk replied. 'But there's still a Mr Maugham waiting here to see you.'

" 'Then please send him up,' I said. "Presently a young man was shown into the room," Willie continued. "And this was Mr Maugham. He had dark curly hair and brown eyes and a sallow complexion. He was obviously sensitive, rather Bohemian and very highly strung. There was a striking family likeness."

Willie paused for dramatic effect—as he always did when telling a story. "But the oddest thing of all about it," he said, "was that the young man spoke with a pronounced stammer."

Willie handed me my glass. "And my visitor told me that the Maughams came over to America a century ago,"

Willie continued. "But the essential characteristics had obviously still persisted in the young man."

Willie took a sip of his drink.

"We're the product of our genes and chromosomes," he concluded. "And there's nothing whatever we can do about it. And that's the reason why I tell you that a psychiatrist couldn't help you. No one can. Because we can't change the essential natures we're born with. We can't alter the essential product that we are. All we can do is to try to supplement our own deficiencies. Meeting that young man in the Ritz-Carlton made me certain of it. There's no point in trying to change. One hasn't a hope."

*   *   *

One of *my* many deficiencies is that I am totally lacking in what is known as "card sense". However, despite my protests, Willie decided that in order to pass our evenings together pleasantly he would teach me to play bridge. The lessons were a trial to me because I could see that my obtuseness was irritating Willie. But worse was to come.

A man and his wife, both of whom were professional and well-known bridge players but whose name—probably for Freudian reasons—now escapes me, came down to Parker's Ferry to visit Willie. He invited them to play bridge with us. By ill-fortune the cards so fell that Willie and I had to play together as partners. However many mistakes there are to be made in a game of bridge—I made the whole lot of them.

Willie glowered at me in silence. "If there's one thing I cannot abide it is wilful stupidity," he said to me after the couple had left. Then he retired to his bedroom.

*   *   *

77

As usual, however ill or depressed he was feeling, Willie forced himself to continue with the habit of work. His discipline was incredible; for each day he would go to the small cottage, near to the house, which had been turned into a writing-room for him. It was here that he had written most of *The Razor's Edge*; it was here he continued to work on his voluminous notebooks—which he had kept since he was a young man and which were eventually to become *A Writer's Notebook* (dedicated to Gerald Haxton). But at that stage Willie was considering writing a book about incidents from the New Testament. He had had several books sent down from New York to help him with his research. He was particularly interested in the Crucifixion.

During his researches Willie had discovered that Mark was the oldest Gospel. "But why does it break off just before the Resurrection?" he would ask. "And in the middle of a sentence? We know that the rest of the work is that of an editor. Why did the author of the Fourth Gospel attempt to attribute the authorship to John Zebeddee if either he was John the Presbytery or a disciple of the latter? Moreover, why are the synoptic Gospels— John especially—so circumstantial about events immediately *prior* to the Crucifixion and so vague after? Why did Peter and Stephen make such a point of connecting Jesus with Jewish Messianic prophecies? Why didn't they shout out: 'This is the only man who ever rose from the dead?' What is odder still is why should Pontius Pilate have given permission to Joseph of Arimathaea to remove the body and put it in a tomb—when he had no personal animosity against Jesus so far as we can see? Like any other Governor he wanted peace. Pilate knew that if the body of Jesus disappeared his followers were bound to make the most of it. The only thing we know about

Joseph of Arimathaea is that he was a rich man. Perhaps he was sufficiently rich to bribe a small provincial Governor. Perhaps the body of Jesus was still living when it was taken down from the cross. You do see; it's quite an interesting idea."*

During my stay at Yemassee I explained to Willie that the doctors had said that my head wound and fits of amnesia made it impossible for me to practise as a lawyer. While I had been in various hospitals for head injuries, Michael Kremer, the specialist, had suggested that I should write the story of my existence in tanks in the Western Desert as a form of occupational therapy. I had followed his advice; and through the good offices of novelist Elizabeth Myers, a friend of my sister Kate, my work had been published in book form—as *Come to Dust* —by Chapman and Hall. The book had had a success with the critics and had sold out within a few days; a paperback edition was about to be produced. I had decided, I told Willie, that my "essential nature" lay in writing. But Willie was no more encouraging to me than his brother Harry had been to him.

"Ner-nonsense," Willie replied. "You'll never make more than £300 a year as a writer. What I advise you to do is to marry a rich woman, ger-go into politics and you'll end up as Governor General of some remote island —which must be a very pleasant existence. Emerald Cunard and I will help you to find an heiress—and the rest is easy."

But I didn't want an heiress; I didn't want to go into politics; and I didn't want to marry. I wanted to be a writer, and I wanted to travel. And I wanted, as Willie

* This conversation was to inspire my novel *The Sign* (W. H. Allen, London, 1974) some thirty years later.

would have put it, to have a romp—when I got the chance.

Willie was now far better; and I returned to England.

*　　*　　*

Willie and Alan Searle, who had become my uncle's secretary and companion in 1945, returned from America to the Riviera in 1946. Willie found that the Mauresque was uninhabitable—for successive waves of troops had each managed to add to the damage already wrought by those who had been there before. First came the Italians, who confiscated Willie's cars; then the Germans converted the villa into an observation post and appropriated the yacht, the *Sara*. When the Allies invaded France the house was fired upon by the British fleet. Latterly, British and American troops had been stationed there. Willie soon put plans for renovation into operation, while he and Alan settled in a small hotel in St Jean Cap Ferrat. I was invited to stay with them in August, when they moved back into the villa.

Willie did not have a car—but in the taxi drive from the airport he told me about the damage he had found at the Mauresque upon his return there.

"Alan and I had a very pleasant journey over, in a small French ship, very clean and sufficiently comfortable," he told me. "And the food was good. There was hardly a ripple on the sea. The passengers were for the most part children of Israel returning to Asia Minor, Hungary, Rumania, Tunis, Morocco, France. Our first impression of France was rather dismal. There was only one custom house official to pass through more than two hundred and fifty passengers—most of them with stacks of luggage. We were kept hanging about the docks for seven hours before we could get away. Such lack of

80

organisation, such slovenliness and incompetence. But at last we did get away and we settled in a small, quite decent hotel, La Voile d'Or at St Jean. The hotel only provides rooms—of which we've had three and a bath-room. We've been paying 600 francs a day, with the *petit déjeuner* thrown in—so it's not been too expensive. We had our meals in a neighbouring restaurant where we eat as well as in a good restaurant in New York and for about the same prices as in New York." Willie paused for a moment and took my hand in his. "My dear Robin, it is so nice to see you again. And you seem so much fitter than you were when we last met."

"I'm feeling much better," I told Willie.

As the taxi sped along, we gazed for a moment in silence at the remnants of war scattered about the road-sides. "Of course," Willie continued, "the villa was in a frightful mess. But not in such a bad state as I had feared it might be. There wasn't a pane of glass in the windows and they tell me that glass at present is all but unobtain-able. The roof is only temporarily repaired, but the damage to the house and the swimming-pool has been patched up and a coat of paint has hidden most of the scars. Moth and rust have corrupted a great deal of what was left, carpets and such like. When I got the furniture out of store, much of it had suffered delapidation . . . but the pictures are all safe, thank goodness," he said. Then he became silent and I felt that he must have been thinking about Gerald who had so cleverly hidden (and buried) so many of Willie's valuable possessions.

"Do you know," Willie said suddenly, "when I asked what had happened to the dogs, I was told they had been eaten long ago."

* * *

The night we moved into the villa, Alan stayed behind to set things in order, Willie and I walked down the road to have drinks with Willie's old friend Bill Sherfesee. Later, as we walked unsteadily back to the Mauresque, I reflected that this was the only time I had ever seen Willie drunk. On that walk, he said only one thing to me: "I shall never get over Gerald's death."

*   *   *

Willie was still a little depressed the following day. "You know I'm now seventy-two," he told me. "At my time of life one finds all one's friends and acquaintances dying like flies around one." Willie smiled at me sardonically. "But perhaps it's just as well," he told me, "for, you see, it does remove further risks of libel actions."

Two of the people he had used as characters in his novels had but recently died; Aleister Crowley—once described by the *Daily Express* as the wickedest man in the world, and Hugh Walpole. Willie had often used real people, with only the thinnest of disguises, as characters in his books and short stories. Often they were furious—the first edition of *The Painted Veil* had to be withdrawn after a libel action was taken, the name of two of the characters changed and the location; occasionally they were flattered—as was "Chips" Channon when he decided that he had formed the basis for the character of Eliot Templeton in *The Razor's Edge*. Crowley, who appeared as the black magician Oliver Haddo in *The Magician*, hadn't been too annoyed, but Walpole had been tremendously upset. I asked Willie about this.

"I don't think Crowley was annoyed at all," Willie told me. "If anything, he was amused. I remember him reviewing the book under the pseudonym Oliver Haddo for one of those publications like *Vanity Fair*. But there was far more trouble with poor Hugh. He threatened to take a libel action. I'm afraid he'd been most upset by my portrait of him as Alroy Kear. Apparently, according to Peter Stern, he'd arrived home from an evening at the theatre and—still dressed in his evening clothes—sat down on his bed and started to read *Cakes and Ale* which had only just been published. It wasn't until he slithered to the floor with an attack of cramp that he realised that he had been reading the book right through—spellbound, I may add—horrified because he recognised certain traits in the character of Alroy Kear as belonging to himself. So he threatened me with a libel action. On the advice of your sainted father, I wrote to Hugh and told him that of course I hadn't meant the character of Kear to be him—that if anything there was more of me in Kear than anyone else. So he dropped the idea. But you know, he put me into a book later*—not that I took any notice of it. I haven't yet admitted in print that Hugh *was* Alroy Kear—but I suppose one of these days I might."† Willie paused for a moment. "It is inevitable that a writer should use people he knows or has observed as the model for characters he is writing in a book—in a way it is a form of flattery; at least it shows that they had some point of interest to attract the writer's attention. But one must always be rather careful, Robin, my dear. Remember that. For though people may be flattered to appear in a book —they hate nothing more than to appear foolish, and will be down upon you like a ton of bricks."

*   *   *

* *John Cornelius: His Life and Adventures* by Hugh Walpole (Macmillan, London, 1937).

† Willie eventually did come clean in print about using Hugh Walpole as Alroy Kear; *Cakes and Ale with a special Introduction by the Author* (The Modern Library, New York, 1950).

I spent most of the next few years travelling in North Africa and various other countries; I lived for a while in Tanganyika. I saw nothing of Willie though we continued to correspond. It was during this time that my father paid a visit to the Mauresque. As I was subsequently to learn from Willie, this visit had hardly been satisfactory.

"It may have escaped your notice," Willie said during dinner on the first night of my next visit to the Mauresque, "but during your absence abroad your sainted father deigned to spend a fortnight as a guest in this house."

"Did he?" I exclaimed in surprise.

"Indeed he did," Willie said. "And he managed to spend fourteen days beneath this roof without passing one single civil remark."

Success over the years mellowed both my father and Willie sufficiently for the two brothers to meet on odd occasions with interest and a certain admiration for their mutual longevity, combined with a solicitude for their health. "We must face it," Willie said to his brother, when my father was ninety and Willie was eighty-three, "we must face it that both of us were endowed with very frail constitutions."

But though they sometimes met quite affably, my father's disapproval of Willie persisted, and my uncle's resentment of my father's attitude grew to violent dislike. Unfortunately neither brother was capable of appreciating the full extent of the other's success—and for this reason: my father was convinced that if he had stooped so low as to adopt the career of a professional writer he would have written far nobler and more eloquent works than Willie; whereas Willie was calmly certain that if he had decided to adopt a political career he would have done better than end up as Lord Chancellor for a year or two. These convictions did nothing to improve the relationship between the two old and distinguished brothers.

My father's visit, I discovered, had been a failure from the very beginning. In those days Willie knew three princesses in Monte Carlo, and when he wanted to impress a guest, Jean, his chauffeur, was sent off to collect them for lunch. They were fetched for my father's benefit, and Annette was given special instructions for the lunch party.

"Tell me, Lord Maugham," said the youngest princess, aged seventy, towards the end of a luxurious meal, "tell me, how do you find the Riviera suits you?"

My father took out his monocle, raised it with a trembling hand to his right eye, looked at the princess for an instant without speaking, and then let the monocle drop from his eye. The dignity with which this ploy was accomplished was such that it reduced the whole table to silence—which was precisely its purpose.

"Does the Riviera suit you?" the princess quavered.

"Yes," replied my father. "I find this plain cooking agrees with me."

The remark did not endear him to his host. Then, while Willie was still silent, the eldest princess addressed my father.

"Your nose is exactly like your brother's," she remarked.

"You mean my brother's nose resembles mine," my father corrected her.

*　　*　　*

On his side, Willie had reasons to dislike my father— and one of them was envy. When shy little Willie was sent at the age of ten to live with his uncle the vicar of Whitstable, my father was the head prefect of Dover

85

College and a member of the rugger fifteen and the cricket eleven. When Willie was being bullied at King's School, Canterbury, because he was bad at games, my father was rowing for Cambridge. When Willie was being cruelly mocked because of his stammer, my father's talent in debate helped him to become President of the Union. When Willie was only making £100 a year as a writer, my father was earning £1,000 a year at the Bar. The year after Willie was divorced from Syrie and decided to leave England, my father became a High Court Judge. The year that Willie was most distressed by the scandal caused by Gerald Haxton's wildly drunken behaviour on board his yacht, my father become Lord Chancellor of England. Willie certainly had reasons for envy.

"Various barristers I've met have informed me that your father was the most brilliant lawyer of our time," Willie said to me. "Unfortunately, when he became Lord Chancellor he treated the peers in the House of Lords as if they were hostile witnesses. So far as I am concerned," Willie continued, "ever since I can remember, during all the years of my life, your father has been beastly to me. He has never had a good word to say to me. I was quite a success. But if we met, your father wouldn't mention even one of my plays. If it hadn't been for your mother I would never even have been asked to the house. She used to say to him, 'Isn't it time we asked Willie to lunch?' Sometimes I'd go and have tea with her when your father was working and we'd have a lovely talk together. But as soon as *he* came in it all changed ... It wasn't until recently that he ever said anything pleasant to me. He did deign to say that some book I'd written recently had something to commend it ..."

Willie unclasped his hands and stretched out his fingers.

"I wonder if he was like that because of your grand-father," Willie continued. "You see, we were orphaned. And your grandfather had lived very extravagantly with carriages and servants, entertaining lavishly. But when he died we were left with only £150 a year... Anyhow your father has never been kind to me. But your mother has. I shall never forget her kindness... I did a portrait of your father's character in a book I once wrote. I think it was called *The Painted Veil*."

It will be observed that the portrait of Bernard Garstin in *The Painted Veil* is far less unkind than Willie's later descriptions of my father.

"Your father bore his time here with grim disapproval. The rich food and good wine he was invited to partake of, and to all appearances enjoyed, brought on a slight attack of guilt which did nothing to lead him to look upon his stay with any greater indulgence," Willie told me. "I could not but feel sorry for him. In the last few months he has grown very, very much older, he is now very frail, and both his movements and his mental pro-cesses have slowed up. Sometimes he seemed almost childish." Willie paused for a moment and gazed at me reflectively. "Oh dear, I do hope I don't go like that. I should hate to see people being tolerant to me because I was so old and rather foolish and allowances must be made for me because of my past."

*   *   *

While I was staying on the farm I had rented in Tanganyika, my novel *The Servant* was published in the United States. James Stern in the *New York Times Book Review* had hailed it is a "masterpiece of writing", unfortunately he had added the fatal words "written with a skill and speed the author's uncle might well envy". My publishers had used this quote in their advertisements. This had enraged Willie and for two or three years I knew I was out of favour.

Willie still led a comfortable life at the Villa Mauresque. He was looked after by Alan Searle, who had been with him constantly since the end of the war. If ever the over-used words "loyalty and devotion" meant anything, Alan Searle exemplified them. There were six servants and four gardeners. The villa ran smoothly. But Willie was an unhappy man; he had become withdrawn and censorious. He disapproved violently of my relationships with various boys. *Now*, I can understand his anger with me at that time because, after all, I had done precisely what he had told me not to do all those years ago at Parker's Ferry. Where was the heiress? Where was my seat in Parliament? How could I end up as the Governor of some colony while leading my present life? Indeed, what was I doing? In Willie's eyes, I was committing two crimes. I was living openly on my little yacht with a boy, and, far worse, I was writing novels which sold well.

One night I was invited alone to dine at the Villa Mauresque. After Gerald's death, Willie seldom gave large parties, but that night there were several guests. In the middle of dinner Willie turned on me in a sudden fit of rage. "Yer-you're making a complete hash of your life," he said. "You'll never be a writer. And do you know how I see yer-your fer-future?" he stammered.

"No, Willie," I answered. "How?"

There was silence round the table. I could see that the guests were extremely embarrassed by Willie's rage. "I see you as an ageing, impoverished Viscount," he told me, "on the fer-fringes of literary society."

I smiled at him. "And do you know how *I* see my

Better night because Henri has given me a flit bomb (scented!) to
combat the mosquitoes. A still ill with his liver complaint, but the
doctor says he's better & has given him liquorice. Why? As a laxative.
Said goodmorning to A (swaddled in blankets in close heat) & went
up to pool. At 11 he appeared: "Ah, then you are! No, don't
get up. Just sit quiet & I'll let you know when it's time for
cocktails." Read Vita's book "La Grande Mademoiselle" overcast.
At 12.30 met in A's room & I showed him photos of my trip to
Moulton & Stamford.
A: "You're both of you late. It's time for cocktails." So down
we went, And at 1245 exactly Maurice brought in & made a
dry martini (with the spray of mint in it)
W: "The Bruntons came over with William the Conqueror." One
of them was beheaded by H8 for being too keen on Anne Boleyn.
But they'd been given land in Ireland that didn't belong to them.
It belonged to the O'Neills. There was a feud. Then the Bruntons
invited all the O'Neills to a banquet & murdered the lot of them.
Their last country house is now a school. They were related to Richard
the Second."
   At lunch (Spanish omelette & loup) on table was a
beautiful pale blue cloth with white embroidery. W: "A & I went
to a convent outside Florence where they make these cloths & I
ordered first 1 & then far more. Then A said 'Hadn't
you better find out how much they cost.' So I asked & when I
found out I said: 'Well, I'll just have this one.'"
   Suddenly W startled me.
   "Has it ever occurred to you to ask yourself what they
feel about you." "Who?"
   "The people who are giving you this food."
   "I think it depends on their country & their people"
   "I can tell you this. They hate the lot of us. They—
   "They may hate us as a class," I said. "But not you
as an individual"
   "One because I punish her for being a ...

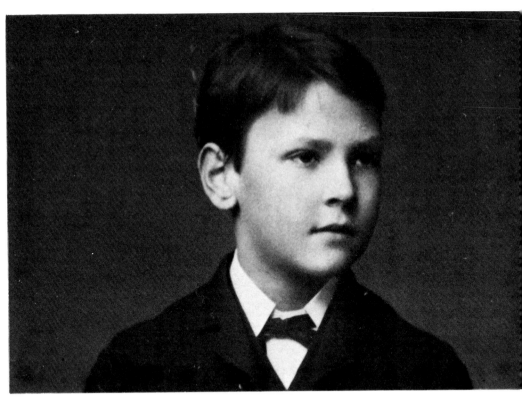

LONDON STEREOSCOPIC

W. Somerset Maugham as a schoolboy, and at age 17

Maugham as a young man

The two brothers, Frederic and William, 1936

CECIL BEATON

Syrie

Liza – Willie's daughter

Gerald Haxton

The author with his uncle at Parker's Ferry, 1945, and at the Villa Mauresque, 1959

e cottage and the writing-room on Nelson Doubleday's estate at Parker's Ferry,
North Carolina

These cartoons by Bernard Partridge and Ronald Searle appeared in 'Punch' in 1908 and 1954

The Moorish sign against the evil eye at the entrance and the front door of the Villa Mauresque

The swimming pool at the Villa

Two studies of Alan Searle, one taken in 1965 with Willie in the garden of the Villa

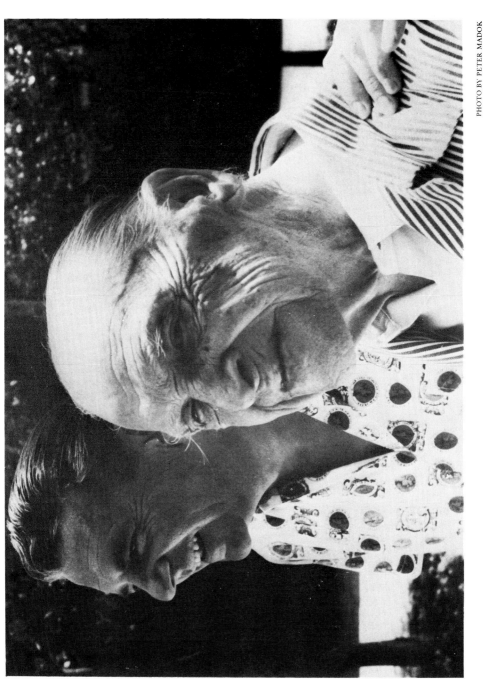

Robin and Willie at the Villa Mauresque, 1965

APIS

Maugham on his ninetieth birthday, and aged 91

The opening of The Maugham Library at The King's School, Canterbury, 1961, and the funeral service

future?" I asked him. To my delight Willie fell into the trap.

"No, he replied. "How do you see it?"

"Precisely the same." I answered.

The guests laughed, but Willie glowered at me.

I went to lunch at the Mauresque a few days later. I was told to come alone. After lunch, Alan left me with Willie. We were sitting on the sofa. Willie clasped and unclasped his hands. "I have a few remarks to make to you," he announced. I was silent. Willie lit a cigarette.

"I her-happen to know something about writing," he began. "You've got to have the knack. But it's more than that... An author doesn't only write when he's at his desk, he writes all day long, when he's thinking, when he's reading, when he's experiencing. He's storing up everything he feels, every person he meets. He's writing when he's eating his breakfast. He's writing when he's making love. It's a full-time job. And it takes up every scrap of energy and brain that he's got."

"So more or less a writer's got to give up everything to be a success?" I asked. "You almost make it sound as if a writer's got to sell his very soul to be a success."

Willie's face was suddenly grim. "I suppose you could put it that way. And I fear, my dear Robin," Willie continued, "that you are unwilling, incapable of or indisposed to make any such sacrifice. I must tell you here and now that you'll never make a writer. I want you to ger-give up the attempt before you make a complete fool of yourself. I also wish you to discontinue your friendship with that common young man. He quite obviously deosn't care a rap for you. He's just out for what he can get."

For a while Willie was silent, then he turned to me once again.

"I realise that you're obstinate," he continued. "I know

also that you're cer-conceited. So I don't expect that you'll listen very carefully to what I have to say. Ber-but I happen to know that you've got very little money apart from what you make from your novels and from journalism—and that can't be very much. Your young friend and that yacht on which you are living are going to ruin you between them. So this is my proposal. If you do what I say—if you give up writing, if you abandon your ler-ludicrous affair with your boyfriend, if you per-promise me that you'll go back to England and marry and settle down to the career of a politician, then I will make over to you £50,000."

"Thank you," I said. "I'm very grateful. But I'd like time to think your offer over."

Willie stubbed out his cigarette. "I have said all I intend to say," he told me. "And now I shall go up to my room for a siesta." He rose from the sofa and walked out of the room. Our meeting was at an end.

The following day Harold Nicolson, by now a close friend of mine, came to stay with me on board my little yacht. Harold was generous and witty. When I was alone with him I told him of Willie's offer.

"Why did you say that you'd think it over?" Harold asked. "Why didn't you tell him that you refuse to be bribed?"

"Perhaps I should have done," I answered. "But I just couldn't face a scene. Sometimes Willie frightens me."

"Well, he doesn't frighten *me*," Harold said, laughing. "I find his hypocrisy rather unpleasant. Did you tell him that I was coming to stay?"

"No," I answered.

"Then *don't* tell him," Harold said. "I don't want to see him."

But Willie heard that Harold had been staying with me.

He was enraged that Harold hadn't called on him. Once again I was summoned to the Mauresque. "I mer-must tell you," Willie said, when we were alone, "that your affair with *that boy* is causing a scandal in Villefranche. In the bars he frequents he fer-flaunts his relationship with you. Everybody in Villefranche knows that you are my nephew, and you're getting me a bad reputation."

I said nothing. Willie was silent. I looked at him. His yellowish eyes were glaring at me. He was a very different person from the man who had lain on my bed in Yemassee sobbing that, now that Gerald was dead, I was the most important person in his life.

"I mer-may also tell you that it's only a question of time before your sainted father hears about the life you're leading. And I certainly wouldn't like to be responsible for the consequences," Willie concluded.

The threat was quite obvious.

*　　*　　*

In 1954, Willie was eighty. Celebrations were world-wide—with exhibitions of his first editions, books and manuscripts in many of the major cities of the world. The crowning moment came when Willie was awarded the Order of the Companion of Honour. After the ceremony, Willie came to my sister's house in Cadogan Square. He showed us the decoration.

"Willie, dear, it's beautiful," Kate said. "How exciting it all is."

"The Order of the Companion of Honour," I said. "It sounds so impressive."

When Willie smiled fondly at me, I could see that he had forgiven me—though I had known it before because he had asked me to dine with him at Boulestin's that evening.

"Even the high-brow papers now rave about you," Kate continued. "Willie, you must be a bit thrilled."

"I've been writing for over half a century," Willie replied, "and yer-you wouldn't have thought it could have taken the critics all that time to realise I can write ... and now it's come too late. I don't care a row of beans what they say."

"Were you ever offered a knighthood?" Kate asked him.

"It was suggested at one moment," Willie answered, "but I declined the idea."

"Why?" Kate asked.

"Because if I went into a party and they announced Mr Arnold Bennett, Mr H. G. Wells, Mr Hugh Walpole, Mr Rudyard Kipling—and Sir William Somerset Maugham —I thought I'd look rather silly."

* * *

Barbara Back and I were sitting in Boulestin's that evening at a table laid for three. Barbara had aged since I met her but her elegance and vitality remained constant. "I'm ravenous," Barbara said. "I wish Willie would hurry up."

At that moment Willie appeared. "I'm ser-sorry I'm late," he said. "But as I was crossing the hotel lobby I was stopped by a woman ... and do you know, for some reason that now escapes me, she was once my wife."

Over dinner we managed to persuade Willie to describe the scene that had just occurred.

He had been moving across the lobby of the Dorchester when a voice called out "Willie". He stopped, then turned slowly. Facing him was an elderly woman, well dressed with chic and elegance. The voice and the gleam in the dark eyes had remained almost unchanged. Syrie moved hesitantly towards him.

"Willie, how are you?" Syrie asked.

"Rising eighty—and rather tired," Willie replied. "How are you, Syrie?" he continued. "You look well preserved."

"Like a jam," Syrie said. "But now the jar's beginning to crack a bit. Shall we sit down?"

They had sat down in an alcove; Willie offered Syrie a drink but she declined. "Today must have pleased you," she said.

"A little . . ." Willie answered. "Did Liza tell you she dined with me last night? It was lovely to see her."

"I'm glad," Syrie stated. "Whatever else I may not have done, at least I produced a child for you."

"Yes . . ." Willie said. "At least Liza survived from the wreck."

"I was sorry to hear about Gerald . . ." Syrie began.

Willie's hands suddenly twitched. "Do you mind," he said, "but I'd rather not talk about it?"

There was a moment of awkward silence.

"You may not have to pay alimony much longer," Syrie announced.

"Der-don't tell me you're going to get married again?" Willie enquired.

Syrie smiled. "No, Willie," she answered. "It was just a way of telling you that I don't think I shall live much longer . . . But I should have remembered that you don't like prevarication."

"You mustn't believe what the doctors tell you," Willie told her. "They're almost as stupid as politicians—and that's saying a great deal."

There was a pause; Syrie spoke very quietly. "When you look back," Syrie said, "don't some of our arguments and upsets seem terribly unnecessary? . . . If only we'd been more understanding, more tolerant of each other . . .

You see, Willie, I believe now that our divorce was a mistake."

"We should never have married," Willie replied. "*That* was the mistake."

Syrie must have flinched at his cold dispassionate voice. "But I was in love with you," Syrie said. "And you swore . . ."

"The tragedy of love isn't death or separation," Willie informed her. "The tragedy of love is indifference . . ."

Willie told us that by this time he was longing to get away. But Syrie had not yet finished.

"There's something I've wanted to say to you these last ten years if I ever got the chance . . ." she murmured. "It's this. I still love you, Willie . . . You must believe that."

"You love a person you've invented over the years called Willie Somerset Maugham," Willie replied. "You don't love *me*—you can't—because you've never known me."

"How can you say that?" Syrie asked.

"I say it, because it's true," Willie said. "And now you must excuse me. I'm dining out this evening and I must go and change."

Willie made a move to go. Syrie rose with dignity. She was close to tears. "We may never meet again," she said. "Won't you kiss me good-bye, Willie?"

Willie spoke with polite indifference. "Yes," he answered. "I'll kiss you." He inclined his face forward and brushed her cheek with his lips. Then he gave a little bow. "Good-bye, Syrie," he said.

"Do you want our farewell to be like that?" Syrie asked.

"Ler-like what?" Willie enquired.

"Like a farewell between two distant acquaintances," Syrie said.

Willie spoke very slowly and very sharply. "I wonder if we were ever anything more," he said.

Syrie died the following year, in 1955.

*   *   *

In December 1956, I developed some mild internal trouble and had to go into the Lindo Wing of St Mary's Hospital, Paddington. Here is an entry from my diary.

"Willie has just left. When he arrived John Sutro was here and Willie greeted him affably. 'I knew you when you were a young stripling,' he said. 'I never see you at the Garrick now,' he continued. 'But perhaps that's because we hurry over lunch and go upstairs to play bridge until three—when those who have work have to leave.'

"John left, squirming with pleasure like a bashful schoolboy.

"After exchanging the usual pleasantries, Willie said, 'Your poor father's mind has gone. His physical health is good and he seems quite happy, but he has lost his mind. Strange to think that such a fine and good brain should go like that ... Thank heavens during the last two or three times I have been to see him Kate has been there so I have been saved The Tour of the Pictures. Every time I used to go to see your father I used to have the ordeal of The Tour Round the Pictures. And you can't imagine how bored I got with those damn pictures.' Willie paused for a moment, and gazed silently at me. 'You know your father really has got a nerve. I don't know if you've seen the new Dutch picture he's bought. It's quite an agreeable, pretty little thing. Of course he paid very little for it. But it's a pleasant enough minor painting. Well—your father rang up the head of all Christie's and asked him to come round and look over it. And what's more—*the man came.*'

" 'If I were younger,' Willie said a little later, 'I would go back to India. There's a mass of material there that has never been used. I'd go to see the Prince of St Asis—Mysore, Hyderabad, Travencore—where there are pleasant and hospitable people. And I'm told that now the English have been hoofed out of there, they quite like us. I'd always travel there by boat because on board you meet people returning to India who have got interesting things to tell you.'

"Willie was always very conscious of how loathed the Imperialist English were in their far-flung colonies. He once commented that he had found the English detested wherever he went in the world because they were 'so class-conscious and sniffy'. This class-consciousness he blamed upon the public-school system—and recollecting that the Battle of Waterloo was said to have been won on the playing fields of Eton, Willie commented that it might be said that India had been lost to the Empire 'in the public schools of England'.

"This was the time of Suez, and Willie and I discussed the political situation. 'Nehru says that Anthony Eden has done Britain a greater injury than any other Prime Minister since Lord North,' Willie commented. 'I have an explanation of why he did it. I have no evidence for it. It's only my own idea. But I have known Anthony for some twenty years... You see, he's an extremely vain man, and I think he thought he was losing popularity with the British public and wanted to do something big to make a splash and bring him back into favour again. In any case, he should never have gone to Jamaica to convalesce—however proud he was. He could have gone to the South of France or Torquay where there's a perfectly good hotel he could have stayed at and enjoyed complete privacy... The only way he can save his face is to get his doctor to say he's too ill to go on. Then the rebels can get what they want—a clean sweep with someone like Duncan Sandys leading the Party.'

"Willie finished speaking. He stood up. 'Well, I must go,' he said. 'I have to see my doctor to try to get some nembutal tablets. I hope you're better soon. *Au revoir, mon cher.*' "

*   *   *

In August 1959, I was once again staying at the Villa Mauresque.

Willie again told with relish the story of a neighbour of his who, when told a newcomer to the Cap was rich, replied indignantly: "Nonsense, I happen to know she wasn't left more than thirty million."

Willie asked his friend why he didn't go into politics.

"Why should I?" his friend replied. "I tell the Ministers what to do as it is."

A man has written to Willie saying: "Since I intend to communicate with you in the next world, perhaps I had better tell you something about myself in this."

Willie said to Alan: "Perhaps I should put an advertisement in *The Times* Personal Column saying 'Mr Somerset Maugham declines to communicate with or be communicated to by *anyone* in the next world'."

*   *   *

Dinner the second night consisted of cold soup, chicken, haricot beans and sliced potatoes, cheese and fruit—some excellent figs, vin rosé. Willie had developed a habit of switching from one subject to another without pause or explanation. Thus he suddenly spoke of Noël. "I wasn't

97

shocked that they slated Noël's ballet*; I was only shocked that the press told me they were going to slate it six weeks before it went into rehearsal."

Then, suddenly, he said, "Karl Pfeiffer's book† was unpleasant and vulgar. He appears to have known me far better than I knew him."

"Tomorrow," Willie said, "Felix Marti-Ibañez, the Editor of *MD*, and his wife are coming to lunch." He stared at me almost defiantly. "And they're coming to see me, not you," he said. "So you can keep quiet and only speak when spoken to."

We were sitting on the terrace when the butler led out Ibañez and his wife. They greeted Willie warmly.

"And this," Willie said, indicating me with a quick nod of his head, "is my nephew Robin."

Ibañez stared at me. "Not Robin Maugham?" he blurted out.

"Yes," I said, dreading what was to come.

"The Robin Maugham who wrote *The Servant, Come to Dust, Behind the Mirror* ...?"

The list seemed to me interminable. Meanwhile Willie had begun to scowl.

"My wife and I have read all of your books," Ibañez continued. "We admire them very greatly."

---

* Noël Coward's ballet to which Willie referred was *London Morning*, composed in 1958 and staged in 1959 by the London Festival Ballet.

† *W. Somerset Maugham: A Candid Portrait* by Karl G. Pfeiffer (Gollancz, London, 1959). In an interview in the *Sunday Express*, Willie, who was determined that no one should write a biography of him, totally dissociated himself from Pfeiffer's book, stating that he had not set eyes on Pfeiffer for ten years and that, in his whole life, he had not "been in his company for ten days'.

Willie's scowl grew heavier. But he made no mention of the conversation later.

At dinner that evening Willie told me he was writing "this and that, a kind of journal, *obiter dicta* about things I haven't had time to write about before. You see," he told me, "I've become so used to writing two or three hours every morning that I don't know how to make the hours go by. But this does the trick... When I've finished it, I shall start writing it all over again because setting it down as I'm doing—just as it comes into my head—it's all muddled, and I want to get it all straight."

Later Alan told me that the "kind of journal" was mainly an account of Willie's life with Syrie—not to be published in Willie's own life-time—terrifyingly bitter, but with the main truth left out.*

Willie did not sleep well last night so I asked if tonight he'd like some of my sodium amytal.

"I don't like taking those drugs for which you have to have a prescription," he said, "because I don't want to get into the habit. But I'll take one just the same."

Willie was then eighty-six. He then told two stories about the Queen of Spain. Willie had admired a pearl that the Queen was wearing and she told him that all the Queens of Spain had worn it. Willie was sceptical—but then he saw the self-same pearl in a painting by Velasquez. On another occasion, Willie went to play bridge with the Queen of Spain. He took £100 with him—not knowing what stakes she played for. "She kept the score in a

* *Looking Back*, Willie's autobiography, has never been published in book form. It appeared as a serial in the *Sunday Express*. ("Rarely, if ever, has a man of his eminence sanctioned publication of such a revealing document during his life-time" proclaimed the *Sunday Express* in the sub-heading to the first episode.) Fuller extracts appeared in America in *Show* magazine.

kitchen account book," Willie told me. "At the end of the evening she turned to me and said, 'Well, Mr Maugham, I'm afraid you owe me 75 centimes.' "

Suddenly the conversation turned to Cairo. Willie pointed to me accusingly. "Robin went to Egypt during the war," he said. "Unfortunately, he was stupid enough to get shot in the head."

Willie then told his favourite story about Winston Churchill. "A small boy was taken by his parents—friends of Lady Churchill—to Chartwell one afternoon in order that he might be introduced to the great man," Willie said, "so that in time he could tell his grandchildren that he had met Sir Winston Churchill. Lady Churchill in her kindness invited the couple and their son—we'll call the boy Tim—to lunch. As they drove to Chartwell, the wife turned to her son and said, 'Now, at lunch you'll be meeting the greatest man alive in the world today.' But Lady Churchill met them at the door with the sad news that Churchill had had one of his attacks and had been told by his doctors he must remain in bed for the day.

" 'I'm very sorry,' Lady Churchill said, 'but at least we can show Tim the goldfish ponds.'

"So after lunch they strolled round the grounds, and Tim admired the famous ponds, and since the husband and wife were great friends of Lady Churchill, they were soon absorbed in conversation and did not notice that little Tim had wandered off. However, they found him waiting by the car.

"As they drove away, the mother turned to her son. 'Tim,' she said, 'I'm awfully sorry you didn't meet the greatest man alive in the world today.'

" 'Oh, but I did,' Tim replied.

" 'No, dear,' his mother said, 'I mean Sir Winston Churchill.'

" 'But I met him,' Tim insisted. 'While you were talking away around the ponds, I went back to the house and I climbed up a huge great flight of stairs and I walked along a great huge corridor, and I came to a great big door—and I opened it. And there, lying in bed, smoking a huge great cigar, was a very, very old man. So I said to him, "Are you the greatest man alive in the world today?"

" 'And he looked up at me, and he said, "Yes, I am— and now you bugger off." ' "

We all laughed. Willie changed the subject again.

"Graham Greene said that one of my plays was the worst he'd ever seen in his life," Willie chuckled. "Of course I retaliated by saying in that case he can never have seen one of his own. And I may tell you he was glad enough to make £50 when I was editing that book of stories* and asked him to make the English collection for me." Willie paused for a moment. "Incidentally," he said, "the play he disliked so much was *The Sacred Flame*. I may sound catty about him, so I'll say this—he still remains the best author writing in England today. They tell me that I should read more modern American authors. But my trouble is that I can't for the life of me understand their language."

* * *

Over lunch the next day one of the guests said to me, "You write very shortly and concisely. Was that due to your uncle's influence?"

I said yes, and explained why.

* *Tellers of Tales: 100 Short Stories from the United States, England, France, Russia and Germany*, Selected and with an Introduction by W. Somerset Maugham (Doubleday, Doran, New York, 1939).

"Ner-nonsense," Willie said, winking at me. "Robin's writing has only been influenced by the Bible."

Alone with Willie earlier in the evening in the garden—where we each had a jigger of whisky "on the rocks"—Willie started to talk about Harry. "He had returned home after a jovial evening with friends," Willie said, "and he made an awful botch of it, you know. He drank nitric acid and was in anguish for three days before he called for someone and we took him to St Thomas's Hospital—where he eventually died." Willie paused for a moment and gazed mournfully at me. "Do you think he was queer?" he asked.

I said I'd always imagined so.

"He was six years older than I was," Willie said, "which makes a great difference. Do you have any recollection of your Uncle Charlie?"

"Yes," I said.

"He was easily the nicest character of the four of us. He was a saint of a man ... but he married that difficult woman."

"Why?" I asked.

"She was eighteen," Willie told me. "She was a fine museum, I mean musician, and her pretty looks and vivacity attracted him."

*   *   *

We dined one night at a small hostelry above Eze. Willie was a little tired, and poor Alan was in pain from his back. Even so, it was a pleasant evening.

We talked of critics. He now despises Cyril Connolly, admires Philip Toynbee, thinks that Harold Nicolson is going off—"But then you must remember that he has drunk heavily all his life," Willie remarked. "And just think of the drudgery of having to produce an article about

102

someone else's book fifty-two weeks of the year as Harold has to in *The Spectator*."

Something seemed suddenly to irritate Willie. "I consider the lights on the way down the pleasantest part of the excursion," he commented.

Willie likes Simon Raven's novel (*The Feathers of Death*) and was glad when I confirmed the authenticity of the background. He thinks *Dr Zhivago* good as a description of Russia but "a lousy novel".

*   *   *

Willie was very lost during the morning and kept arriving at the pool and asking questions such as "How do you spell 'Shah' in the 'Shah of Persia'?" or "Do please look at this signature. Do you think it's Malcolm Sergent or Malcolm Muggeridge? Or perhaps it's Momo Marriott."

When we met for cocktails at 12.45 the atmosphere was charged. "The doctor's an old fool," Alan said.

"Then would you like us to send for a specialist?" Willie asked.

"No, I don't want a specialist," Alan answered. "I just want sense. Why shouldn't I eat eggs? I'm not getting half enough to eat here."

Willie gave a sardonic little smile. "Do you know what makes me think you're better?" he said. "Yesterday you were right down. Today you're aggressive. That's a very good sign."

*   *   *

At lunch I told Willie that my father's official biographer wanted to meet me.

"I'm glad he didn't ask to meet *me*," Willie announced. "As I've told you, the lawyers I've met amongst the peers told me that he was the most brilliant lawyer of our time ... When he became Lord Chancellor he treated the peers as if they were hostile witnesses. But so far as I am concerned—during all the years of my life until I was eighty, he was beastly to me. He never had a good word to say for me. In 1907 I had four plays running at the same time in London. I was quite a success. But your father wouldn't even mention any of them."

Willie looked across the table at me. "He was always beastly to me," he said. "If it hadn't been for your mother I would never have been asked to the house. She used to say, 'Isn't it time we asked Willie to lunch?' Sometimes I'd go and have tea with her when he was working and we'd have a lovely talk together. But as soon as he came in, it all changed.

"It wasn't until I was eighty that he ever said anything pleasant to me ... When I was eighty he did deign to say that some book I'd written recently had something to commend it. I always wonder if he was like that because of our father who lived with carriages and servants, entertaining lavishly. But when he died we were left with £3,000 each. And that came from a country house he was building and some ornaments he'd collected."

Willie now looked very old. His face was lined and the colour of parchment. His fading eyes looked out on the world without any illusion and without much interest, for he had seen it all so many times before. His hands and feet were small, and he seemed somehow to have shrivelled (Willie had always resented his short stature and felt that an additional three or four inches would have made his whole life different), but he moved with dignity and his gestures were full of authority. In the evening, when he had changed into a double-breasted, quilted smoking-jacket and black trousers, and put on his black velvet shoes with his monogram stitched on the toes in gold braid, he looked ancient, fragile, wise and benign, and—you would have thought to look at him—wholly detached from the trivial problems of the world.

But Willie was not detached, and he did not wish to leave the world; he was afraid of death. He made every effort to keep alive; he sometimes went to a clinic in Switzerland where he was injected with goat hormones which the doctor in charge, Niehans, believed prolonged and rejuvenated life.

"Ner-now, Noël Coward is coming to stay tomorrow," he told me one morning. "And I don't want him to know I've had a goat."

"There's no reason why he should know," I replied comfortingly.

That night at dinner Noël leaned forward to me. "I must tell you that your uncle really is a remarkable man," he said. "This afternoon he took me for a walk up the mountainside, and there he was hopping and skipping from boulder to boulder like a mountain goat."

There was an awkward silence.

*   *   *

When Willie was in London, he almost always stayed at the Dorchester. I often lunched with him there and I have deliberately joined together some of these occasions.

*   *   *

In May 1961 I lunched once again with my uncle at the Dorchester. Alan, on this occasion, had gone out to lunch. The finely traced lines of Willie's face, combined with the Oriental slant of his eyes, now gave him the appearance of a Chinese mandarin. In fact, many people have suggested that the Maughams must have sprung from Far

Eastern lands, but I have traced the family back as far as I can, and I find no indication of it. Certainly Willie's clothes that day reminded me of some retired Chinese official. He was dressed in an old quilted grey jacket with a blue scarf wrapped loosely round his throat, and blue floppy worsted trousers. He embraced me decorously and walked towards the chest that contained the drinks.

"Cocktail shakers are wretched implements," he said. "They never work properly and these glasses are so small that we can have a refill and not feel ger-guilty about it." He handed me a dry martini. "Martinis should never be shaken," he said. "They should always be stirred so that the molecules lie sensuously on top of each other . . . Now sit down quietly," he said, "and don't talk so much."

"But I haven't said anything," I answered.

"Well you have now," he replied sitting down next to me on the sofa. "You know age is quite ruthless," he continued. "This morning I was at Gerald Kelly's studio because he's doing another portrait of me. I thought he looked quite haggard. But I expect *he* thought I looked as old as sin.* Gerald Kelly is very pleased with himself because it seems there are various American buyers who are prepared to pay any price for portraits or sketches of me. And I must say I'm very pleased with myself."

"Do you know who are the purchasers?"

---

* Sir Gerald Kelly, K.C.V.O., P.R.A. (1879–1972) first met my uncle at the turn of the century, in Paris—where Willie also first encountered Aleister Crowley and Arnold Bennett. Willie and Gerald Kelly were to remain lifelong friends and Kelly did several portraits of Willie. The most famous of these portraits, "The Jester", hangs in the Tate Gallery, London. A charming portrait of the friendship between the two men appears in Derek Hudson's *For Love of Painting: The Life of Sir Gerald Kelly* (Peter Davies, 1975).

"No," Willie answered. "Well, I'm aware that my new friend Beaverbrook wants one for his museum. Did you know that Beaverbrook was my new friend?"

"He must be fascinating," I said.

"He is, and he seems to be quite fascinated by me," Willie told me. "He's got a crush on me. But I'm eighty-seven and he's eighty-three; so I think it's rather unlikely, don't you? But I'm very flattered all the same."

Willie got up to refill our glasses.

"I think you will enjoy your trip to the South Seas," he told me. "I, too, was in Fiji, but it was shortly after the First World War, so I expect it's all changed since then."

I asked Willie if he was still working on his autobiography. He shook his head. "I'm afraid that my autobiography reveals me in such an unpleasant light that it can't be published until after my death," he said.

We talked about various eccentric friends in the Far East.

"In Siam they're sensible," Willie stated. "They don't regard homosexuality as anything abnormal. They accept it as something perfectly natural ... One day it will be realised that there are people who are *born* homosexual or bisexual and there's nothing whatsoever they can do about it. I'm bisexual, but for the sake of my reputation I don't care to advertise the fact. But as you know, I've loved girls and I've loved boys—I've loved women and I've loved men.

"I think you're right to make a separate trip to Japan," he said suddenly. "I heard an astonishing story when I was in Tokyo ... There was an American banker who had a young Japanese friend, a boy of about eighteen. The boy was devoted to him, and they lived together, but their relationship became so notorious about town that

107

the American banker's employers came to him and told him that the scandal was such that he must break with the boy for once and for all—or be sacked. So that evening the banker sadly broke the news to his friend, and invited him out for a farewell dinner. After dinner they went back to his apartment. And the boy asked the banker, 'Are you certain we've got to part?'

"And the man said 'Yes'.

"And the boy asked 'For good?'

"And the man said: 'I'm afraid so.'

"And the boy took out a knife and plunged it into his stomach and disembowelled himself."

Willie lit a cigarette. "You know, that was really true love. Really true love ... I've met the man. And you'll meet him if you go there."

The waiter wheeled in a trolley. Willie stubbed out his cigarette and we seated ourselves at table. The waiter served us with *oeufs en cocotte*. "I'm half way through your book *The Slaves of Timbuktu*," Willie said. "I find it most interesting. I hope you'll write a book about the Far East. You've learned to write plainly," Willie paused. "But you don't spend enough time on your books. The book would have been ten times as good if you'd cut a third of it and worked harder on the rest of it. What's more, you talk too much about yourself. I can give you a specific example because it struck me at the time. You say at one moment: 'I was sitting in a deck-chair.' But who *cares* what you were sitting in? Nobody cares a fer-fuck. So why put it in? You seemed to give up trying a third of the way through ... Your old girl-friends have done you a lot of harm ... Peter Stern didn't give a damn about your work, she just wanted to get into what she supposed was high society through meeting your mother ... But don't let me depress you. After all, you can go quite a way with very little talent. Noël Coward has little talent but he's made it go a ler-long way . . . So has that man who wrote *The Loom of Youth* . . ."

"Alec Waugh."

"Yes. He writes long books that few of us read but they're very successful. And he's an extremely pleasant person. And he's very kind. *Far* nicer than his brother who I think is quite odious . . . You must realise that I have only come a long way because I have talent. And my success has brought me a number of advantages."

Suddenly Willie looked old and tired. "But I've paid for my success—every bit of it," he told me. "You must never forget that. I've paid for it through my stammer . . ."

The waiter wheeled in a dish of double lamb chops.

"If you want to have a success you must stop doing little things," Willie said. "You must give something more than you're doing at the present. If you want to carry on with politics—and as you know your maiden speech in the House of Lords had a certain success—why don't you try to find some rich politician and set up house with him as his companion? We both know people who've got to the top in that way . . . But the trouble is that you've been very extravagant. Three houses and all that . . . I don't say you're extravagant *now*. But you have been wildly extravagant. And you've only got yourself to blame . . . You haven't been stupid. But you've been vain . . . But we've all made our mistakes. And we've all suffered for them . . . I think if you want to write something that's striking, you should go to India or perhaps to that island in the south of India . . . Yes, Ceylon. I believe you could write a very interesting book about Ceylon— if you go there and watch the people and really *look* at them. You've got to be able to see them properly. And even if you can't find a story, you could always write a book called 'Winter in Ceylon' or something like that. Or you could try Madagascar . . . You've got to *look* at what's going on—not only around the whole world but in England. Your sister Diana took me round the slums of Paddington last week. I'm too old to write about it now. My gift has gone. I'm just a wreck . . . a very imperfect, tormented creature. But if you were to spend a few days with those people in their terrible squalor I believe you could write a book which would shock the whole country."

The waiter brought in a Stilton; Willie thanked him.

"I'd like to end this conversation on a serious note," he continued. "So I'll say this. All over the world there are wonderful stories to be written if only you've got the balls to write them."

For a moment he stared at me in silence.

"I suppose you still think it's a splendid thing to be a success. Ber-but I can tell you this, you can have no idea of how many disadvantages there are to being famous. To give you one example—people only invite you to a party so that they can show you off. In Singapore Alan got ill so I called in a doctor who cured him. And when I asked the doctor how much I owed him he said 'Nothing'. He was only too glad to have been able to help my friend. And he said that it would give him and his wife great pleasure if we would dine with them that night. So I accepted. And they sent a car for us at seven, and we drove out of the town for miles. We must have driven for nearly an hour. And at last we arrived at the doctor's house to find they'd invited all Singapore society to meet us. All the ladies were in long dresses with all their jewels on. All the men were in black ties. And we stood about drinking; I was introduced to one person after another. At eleven Alan went to our host and asked when we were going to have dinner. And the host said, 'Oh, about mid-night, I expect.' So Alan said I was very old and must eat at once . . . But they wouldn't do anything about it; so we left their house and went back to the hotel and dined there quietly . . . You see, people simply want to show me off. They don't really care a fer-fuck about me. And now I'm famous everybody wants to meet me. People I haven't seen for thirty years write letters saying 'Darling Willie, we must meet'. All of them think they're the only pebble on the beach."

The waiter brought coffee. Willie thanked him once again and pressed a tip into his hand. "Do you know sometimes when I look at my stories I can't imagine how they came to be written," Willie announced.

"But all the same," I said, "for all the disadvantages, it must be satisfying to do something better than anyone else in the world."

Willie laughed. "I must confess I'd never thought of it in that light before," he replied. "Though now you mention it I have to admit that I do see your point. But it doesn't give me any pride and it doesn't give me any pleasure. And being so famous has such a lot of disadvantages."

We moved from the table and settled again on the sofa. "I've read the manuscript of your book *The Wrong People*," Willie said. "The descriptions of Tangier are excellent and the characters all come to life. It's the best thing you've ever done."

Willie leant back on the sofa and clasped and unclasped his hands. Then he turned to me. "But, having said that, I must tell you that if you publish the book in this country, it will kill you stone dead. You would completely destroy the reputation you've built up. I think there would be an outcry in the press. And it would ruin you. I've discussed it with Noël and he agrees with me. I'm aware that Cyril Connolly likes the book so much that he's offered to write an introduction to it. I'm also aware that some of your queer friends have urged you to publish and be damned. Equally I happen to be aware that you haven't got a penny piece in the world apart from what you earn from your writing. You may think I'm being old-fashioned, but I happen to know the public better than you do. I know their likes and dislikes. That's why I'm a bestseller throughout the world. Why proclaim from the roof-tops that although you like hopping into bed with girls, you are predominantly homosexual?"

"I've hardly done that," I protested. "After all, it is a novel."

"Do you think anyone could write such a book about the queer life that goes on in Morocco without having experienced it? Do you suppose for one moment that anyone could describe sex with boys in such detail as you do if he hadn't experienced it? Of course, no one could. You write with expert knowledge because you've experienced that way of life for several years ... Do you seriously imagine that, apart from a handful of queers, the public are going to be interested in the goings-on of a few pederasts in Tangier? The public will dislike the book. The critics will slay you and you'll lose such sales as you've got at present. Why do you think that Noël or I have never stuck our personal predilections down our public's throats? Because we know it would outrage them. Believe me—I know what I'm talking about. Don't put your head in a noose—even though it may gain you a tawdry success with some of your friends."

"Thanks for your advice, Willie," I said. "I'm glad you're so definite about it. I'll tell my agents not to publish it here. But I may publish it in America where they're more tolerant."

Willie stared down at his hands for a moment. "You know the novel's extremely well done," he said. "But the interesting thing is—and I don't know whether you realise quite what you've done—you've shown that homosexuality simply doesn't work. In the still watches of the night I've thought it over, and I think you might write another kind of novel . . . Alan had two friends who were devoted and happy and rich, and they'd lived together for years. One evening one of them went upstairs and killed himself. His friend never knew why. And a few years later *he* killed *himself* . . . Now that would make a very interesting homosexual novel . . . but I would never dream of writing it."

Willie got up and went to the telephone and ordered the Rolls he had hired during his stay in London. "You're on my way," he told me. "So I'll give you a lift home."

Suddenly he bent down and kissed me on the head. "Don't be angry with what I've said, it's all for your own good," he murmured.

While we were waiting outside the hotel for Willie's car, a huge Rolls drove up.

"There's my car!" Willie exclaimed, moving towards it. But out got an over-dressed, heavily made-up woman of about fifty, glittering with diamonds and escorted by a tall, handsome man, young enough to be her son but whose proprietary attitude proclaimed that he wasn't. The woman recognised Willie and rushed up to him.

"Willie!" she gushed enthusiastically. "Willie, it's divine to see you and looking so well."

Willie looked at her blankly.

"I'm feeling very old and rather cold," he said at length.

"You look simply wonderful!" she cried. Willie stared at her in silence.

Suddenly doubt assailed her.

"You *do* remember me, don't you?" she asked nervously. "I'm Mabel Swope. I was Mabel Anstey from Johannesburg."

"I'm sorry to hear you've lost all your money," Willie said suddenly.

The woman started as if she had been stung by a viper. "Lost my money!" she exclaimed. "I can assure you I haven't."

"I heard you'd ler-lost every cent," Willie stated firmly.

"I can assure you that you've got that completely wrong," the woman replied with a fixed smile. Then she swept away on her friend's arm.

"Who on earth was she?" I asked.

"I haven't the foggiest idea," Willie answered.

"But then why did you tell her you'd heard she'd lost every cent?"

"Ber-because she was obviously a tiresome bitch," Willie announced, "and she looked too pleased with herself."

At that moment Willie's hired Rolls drove up.

"Get in," Willie said, "and I'll take you home."

"I must tell you," he said when we had settled ourselves in the car, "I must tell you that because of some quirk in my character I have always disliked people who are self-satisfied. The nature of men and women—their *essential* nature—is so vile and despicable that if you were to portray a person as he really is, no one would believe you. Since time began, the life of man has been nasty, brutish and short and, on the whole, it still is. In my writing I have gone quite far in describing human nature as I see it. And for this reason I'm known as a cynic. I'm accused of concentrating on the weaker side of my fellow beings.

But I've tried to be honest. The greatest rule in a writer's work is to beware of cant. They call me a cynic, but I promise you that I'm as moved by virtue as anyone is. I have seen selfless and brave actions by human beings that have reduced me to tears. I believe in love. I believe in altruism—though I'm unable to practise it myself."

Willie was silent for a moment. I wondered if I knew any of the people to whom he was referring.

"Deep in my heart I am a sentimental old party," Willie said. "So now you know the truth."

$$* \qquad * \qquad *$$

In April 1962 Willie, accompanied by Alan, had driven in his Rolls to Lausanne where he was staying in the Hotel Beau Rivage before entering Dr Niehan's clinic.

"I must tell you," he said during my visit, "that Alan is also being treated by Professor Niehans—it gives me such confidence when he goes in immediately before me. Recently we went to see Niehans and he asked Alan if his last treatment had been successful. 'Very,' Alan replied. 'In what way?' Niehans asked. 'Well,' Alan answered, 'when I walk through a field of cows now—they all moo.'"

Willie asked me to stay with him as his guest. Before I left, Noël Coward very sweetly telephoned me in London and asked me to stay with him.

"I shall come across myself to rescue you from that old monster," he said. "You will be positively exhausted after three or four days, so I shall come over while he's having his siesta and whisk you away to my chalet above Montreux."

I thanked Noël, and booked a ticket to Lausanne. Alan met me at the airport and we drove to the hotel. My bedroom overlooked the yacht harbour and the great lake and the vast snow-capped mountains beyond. In the sitting-room adjacent, Willie was playing patience at a small green baize-topped table that seemed to appear by magic wherever he went. He was looking pale but far less strained than in London, and he looked less haunted. He was dressed in a russet-brown tweed jacket and a floppy brown and white tie, light suede shoes and grey flannel trousers.

We embraced and Willie said, "Sit yourself down," as he always did, and asked where I'd been staying. At that moment two enormous mounds of post arrived, both for him and for Alan, who gave Willie a long silver paper-knife. Willie lit a cigarette and they began their task of going through the mail, exchanging remarks as they opened each letter.

"Rosamund Lehmann wants some money for destitute women," Willie said.

"The Rt Hon the Viscount Field Marshal Lord Montgomery wants £10,000 for a pet cause of his and please could you reply immediately," Alan announced.

"He's got a nerve," Willie said. He handed Alan the letter he had been reading. "Who is this woman? I can't read her writing."

"A young American writer in Vienna is being thrown out of his lodgings next week unless he gets some money," Alan said.

And so it went on.

Sometimes Willie would ignore these appeals for money; sometimes he would be so touched by a letter that he was almost ridiculously extravagant.

Alan suggested a walk; Willie suggested a whisky and Alan went off to get it. "I have now been ordered by my doctors to take two or three whiskies a day, neat or on the rocks," Willie told me. "I have one in the morning and another about this hour. My doctors tell me it's very good for me. Whisky softens the arteries, they tell me. It keeps them from going hard... You must remember that I'm now a very very old man."

"You look fine," I said.

"I feel fine on the whole," Willie said. "But one might almost say I was kept going by whisky."

We had a wonderfully happy talk about our mutual friends and then at seven Willie left to lie down. We met at 7.45 and walked along the corridor which led to the lift—and then down a longer corridor to a bar, where a pianist was playing. We dined under a vast cupola with frescos on the ceiling—so much like a church that it seemed almost blasphemous to have turbot and entrecôte and cheese and to drink light white wine. But Willie found the service slow. He suddenly became enraged, first with the waiter and then with the head waiter. *"Un peu de service et vite s'il vous plait,"* he shouted. Willie's rage made me realise that his nerves were still on edge.

We walked back to the lift. Alan and I each took an arm and led Willie, happy and benign again, along the corridor to the living-room.

*   *   *

At eleven the following morning Willie signed some of the first editions of his work I'd brought out. A heap of them. "I don't know who wrote these books," Willie said. "I'm sure I never did."

Presently we went for a walk with Alan along the waterside and then into the public garden which was almost empty except for a young Japanese boy, bespectacled, reading intently on a bench whom we passed just as Willie was talking about his trip to Japan. "They bought me lock, stock and barrel, you know," Willie said.

117

"They were all over me. I've never had such a success."

After a while we sat on a bench and stared across the lake. Willie turned to Alan. "Was it in the First War or the Second War that I was in Geneva?" he asked.

"The First," Alan told him. "When you wrote your Ashenden stories."

"Oh yes. I remember. I used to take secret messages across the lake to the French in Evian."

"Weren't you frightened?" I asked.

"Very," Willie said. Then he laughed. "But it wasn't really all that dangerous. The Swiss were my main danger. But even if I'd been caught they'd have only put me in prison for two years. You see, the Swiss were neutral..."

This reminded me of a question I'd wanted to ask Willie for ages. "What were you doing in Samoa in 1915?" I asked.

For a moment Willie's brow wrinkled in perplexity. "Oh, yes. I remember," he said. "You see, both Australia and Germany wanted to invade Samoa, and there was quite a lot of trouble going on in that area." That was all.

*   *   *

Two tall redwood trees stood outside the hotel which was built in two sections, the older section—about 1908 —being joined by the basilica of a dining-room. Magnolias dripped their white petals onto the green lawn with yellow gorse bushes. There were lily ponds and statues. The trees were filled with delicious pale spring buds. The air was clean and bracing.

Back in the hotel room, Willie said, "I feel very tired. I need my whisky." Alan brought him a double whisky from the bar. While he sipped his drink Willie told me the story of a foreign millionairess on Cap Ferrat who had asked him how she and her husband could get into

English Society. "By owning racehorses," Willie told her. And he was right. "Another rich friend of mine," he continued, "was in a coma. He woke up and saw his family around his bed. 'What day is it?' he asked. 'Derby Day,' they replied. 'Then put £5,000 on Psidium,' he said; then fell back into his coma. His family thought he was raving and did nothing about the bet. A fortnight later the man came out of his coma. 'What day is it?' he asked again. They told him. 'Who won the Derby?' he asked. 'Psidium,' they told him, 'but we thought you were raving at the time so we didn't back it.' 'You bloody fools,' the man said and lay back on the pillows and promptly died.

"Another neighbour of mine on Cap Ferrat," he said, "had a close friend who owned several horses. She was the man's mistress. He assured her that a particular horse would win at the next major race meeting. So the woman —who believed her lover implicitly—sold her shares and her jewellery and put all the money on the horse to win. The horse came in first by a head. She made £60,000 ... and she's never gambled since."

Over his whisky later that day Willie became deliciously mellow and in his old form. Of another wealthy neighbour he said: "Her father was so disgusted to hear that she was a lesbian that he only left her fifty million"—pounds, I presumed.

"Has it ever occurred to you to ask yourself why your father was so very nasty?" Willie asked me suddenly, changing the subject.

I was silent. I knew what Willie was going to say.

"I think it was because of his poverty in his early days," he said. "He was constantly alarmed that he would not be able to maintain his family amongst the 'clean decent people' with whom he liked to associate." Willie took a swig of his whisky.

119

He was very happy, and his mind wandered from subject to subject. "You know, when I was last in London I suddenly wanted some sleeping-pills," he said, "but I hadn't got a doctor handy, so I wrote out a prescription myself and signed it. I rather think it's the only prescription I've ever made out in my life." Willie paused for a moment; he placed his empty whisky glass carefully on the low table in front of him. "Alan took the prescription to Savory and Moore in South Audley Street. They gave him the pills—and I'm told they've framed the prescription."

Willie chuckled and then sighed. "You know my father must have been a very unusual man. Did I ever tell you that at his death it was discovered that during all the years he was a solicitor to the Embassy in Paris he never charged them a penny for his work. And has it ever occurred to you to ask yourself why your father was so very nasty?" —he kept repeating himself in this way—"I think it was the poverty of his early years at the Bar when he was terrified that he would not make enough money to support his wife and family."

*   *   *

That evening I took Willie and Alan to dine at the Grappe d'Or restaurant which I had been told was the best in Lausanne. Willie said that, as I was his guest, he must pay, but I refused. So then he and Alan began to tease me about how much the meal would cost.

"I hope you have got plenty of travellers' cheques on you," Alan said.

"I'm feeling very hungry this evening," Willie said. "Aren't you, Alan?" Then he winked.

We had a delicious meal—caviar on toast, langoustine

thermidor and a Champagne ice which none of us had ever tasted before—a water ice made of Champagne.

Speaking of money, Willie maintained—quite wrongly —that he'd never seen any of the films which had been made from his novels, short stories and plays. He was surprised at the prices paid for film rights.

He displayed a great interest in the couple who were sitting at the next table—a middle-aged Frenchman with a face so plain as to be almost ugly, and a very beautiful girl who was obviously his mistress. Presently the man left the table—presumably either to make a telephone call or to go to the lavatory. "She is beginning to get very cross," Willie said. "She'll give him hell when he gets back, I can tell you that."

But the girl didn't give her lover hell; she smiled at him most sweetly. Both Alan and I looked at Willie to see how he would take the reversal of his prognostication. He was undisturbed. "He must be paying her a lot of money," Willie said.

*   *   *

The following day after breakfast, as he smoked his pipe, Willie said it would be amusing to go to the castle at Chillon—"the castle that Byron wrote his poem about", he explained. "It's roughly an hour's drive from here." Alan and I agreed.

"After we left you in the old town last night, did you enjoy yourself?" Willie asked me.

"Yes," I said. "Enormously." And I told him about my escapades.

"Oh," Willie announced in a disapproving voice. I could see that he was no longer interested in that kind of story.

We drove to Chillon in the Rolls—the suspension of

which seemed in need of attention. "The man who's driving us," Willie said, "is a very odd creature. He's never interested in scenery—only in the car. Outside the Alhambra in Spain I told him I'd pay his entrance fee if he wanted to go in. 'No thanks,' he said, 'I can always buy a postcard.' I should tell you that he's now been with me for over thirty years."

At the castle of Chillon we walked through the lower storeys of the dungeons. "We could turn this into a gymnasium," Willie said.

On the way back to the hotel Willie leaned forward to me, "Do you think the man who lived there thought of it as a retreat?" he enquired. "You see, I know all about ivory towers. An ivory tower is a place into which a man will retire to think of the world in general and himself in particular."

Willie leaned back in his seat and smiled sardonically. For some reason on that day he seemed less deaf and more spry. Back at the hotel, on the way down to lunch, we passed a lace bodice in one of the display windows along the corridor. Willie examined it for a while in silence. Then he turned to me: "I think that's rather *you*," he said. He was certainly in an unusually frivolous mood. After a lunch of terrine, Porterhouse steak, and apple pie, Willie was still more relaxed. On the way up in the lift he said: "I think I'm going straight to bed."

"I'm going there too," I said.

"You might at least wait until you're asked," Willie told me.

He was still happy at tea-time, and plugged away at one of his favourite themes.

"As I've told you," he said, "your father was one of the most odious men I've ever met in my life."

I had thought that my father's death might soften

Willie's animosity towards him. Obviously it hadn't had that effect.

"When he came to stay with me at the Mauresque where, as you know, one end of the living-room is lined from floor to ceiling with books, your father looked at the rows of books carefully. Then he turned to Alan—'Where does my brother keep his books?' he asked. 'Has he no library?' Later Alan asked him what he thought of the living-room. 'Rather a lot of gilt . . .' he said. But he was always like that.

"Fairly recently, after a revival of a play of mine— *Lady Frederick* at the Savoy Theatre—which happened to have quite a success, all the way back in the taxi your father complained to your mother that he hadn't had the financial success in life that I have had . . . But my favourite story about him was when your father appeared at breakfast in full evening dress with all his medals on. Apparently he was going to have his portrait painted by Mr Gunn. Your dear sister Kate drove your father to the address he'd given her. To her surprise, they were shown into a large waiting-room. Eventually, the truth dawned on Kate. Mr Gunn was your father's dentist—and there was your father sitting, dressed in his full regalia."

* * *

The following afternoon Willie took me for a walk alone. He strolled up the hotel garden and through a small door beside a potting-shed, over a lawn strewn with blossom, up a private drive, across a private garden— plodding onward determinedly but not knowing where he was going until at last, thank heavens, we reached the public gardens. Willie loves watching the children slide down the metal chute—"on their little bottoms". I took several photographs of him.

"This place is all right," Willie said. "The air is wonderfully exhilarating and I sleep well. The only trouble is that it's deadly dull ... You know, I've written my autobiography ... but the publishers said: 'We'll publish it if we can take out this part and that part.' But I said: 'No. If you won't publish all of it, then you won't publish it if we can take out this part and that part.' But libel the dead? I didn't, but I really don't much care."

Back at the hotel for tea, which he takes without sugar but with a fresh slice of lemon with each cup, we talked about my family book and later about Willie's work.

"Alan says the valuable collector's items are *A Man of Honour*; *The Hero*; *Orientations*; *The Bishop's Apron* and *My South Sea Island*," Willie told me. "In Madrid," he continued, "my publisher had made a bit of a splash for me. He asked me to come in and sign copies of my books for him at six in the evening. The street was crowded; at nine o'clock I said I was so tired I couldn't go on. But he said: 'There are people out there who have been waiting for three hours and if you leave now there will be a row.' So I had to stay."

*　　*　　*

Alan and Willie would break their bread from breakfast and put it on a little iron table on the balcony for the birds. From the balcony there was a view down into the little harbour where there were a few yachts and some small speed-boats, a cabin-cruiser and the large white steamers that cross over to Evian and move along the shore to Geneva. Beyond the harbour was the lake—so vast it sometimes was easy to think it was the sea. On the far side of the lake rise the snow-capped mountains of the Alps.

The next morning Willie was staring out at the bright

beds of flowers—red tulips, yellow pansies, golden broom, waxen-petalled magnolias and copper beeches. "You know, I used to cross that lake when I was in Intelligence," he said. "I must confess to you that I wasn't very good at the job. Why they chose me—a year or two later—to go to Russia I shall never understand . . . I made a terrible hash of it. I had vast sums of money at my disposal and Kerensky became quite a friend of mine. He always looked very unhealthy. He used to come and see me and stay for hours at a time . . . My whole purpose was to keep Russia in the war. One morning I was awoken and told that Kerensky wanted to see me immediately. I dressed and went round. Kerensky said that he'd got a secret message for Lloyd George—so secret that he daren't put it on paper. He told me what it was. I went back to England on a destroyer, travelling from Oslo to some harbour in the west of Scotland. I went by train down to London and I had a meeting with Lloyd George. As soon as I came into the room I realised that for some reason— possibly the demand for support—he didn't want to know what my message was. He told me how much he'd enjoyed my plays and how glad he was of the opportunity of meeting me. He was very affable. Then I produced the message that I'd written out in the form of a memorandum. He read; he remained silent. Then at last he said: 'I can't.' I said: 'What am I to say when I return to Russia?' 'Just tell them I can't,' he said. Then he added: 'I did so enjoy your last play . . . Now, if you will excuse me, I'm late for a Cabinet meeting.'

"But I never did return to Russia because by that time the Kerensky government had fallen. Then I was summoned to Downing Street; the nobs asked me to read out my memorandum on Russia. But because of my stammer I asked Willie Wiseman, who was our Intelligence agent in America, to read it for me ... You can have no idea what a disadvantage my stammer was to me when I was a secret agent. If I had read out that memo, it might have made all the difference. If I'd been more efficient Russia might have stayed in the war ... Then they told me they were afraid Rumania was in danger: they asked me to go out to do the same job there. But I felt it was only right to tell them that I'd got tuberculosis. So one of them—I think it was Reading—said I ought to go up to Scotland and get cured. Three days later I went ... But I always regret not having gone to Rumania. It would have made a difference to the whole war. And perhaps if I hadn't made a hash of it in Russia, the whole world would be different ... I had hundreds of thousands of pounds in a bank. At the end of the war they asked about it, so I gave it back to the Foreign Office. But the Americans weren't interested."

*   *   *

The next morning Alan was sorting out fan letters; Willie seemed to be dozing in an armchair. At that moment the main door leading to the suite was flung open. Willie looked up anxiously, then he smiled with pleasure as he saw that his visitor was Noël Coward, for he could still enjoy the company of an old friend and he enjoyed bantering with him. Noël walked swiftly across to Willie and embraced him. "My darling Willie," he cried, "*cher maître.*"

Noël then turned to me. "Robin, my dear boy," he said, "lovely to see you."

"What a surprise!" Willie exclaimed.

Noël walked across the room and stared out on to the balcony at the iron table with the crumbs. He turned to Willie, "I suppose the crumbs are for Robin," he said.

126

"Well, I was passing in front of the very gate of this hotel, so I thought I'd just pop in," Noël told us. "Now you may *suppose* that I've only come in for five minutes."

"That's what I was hoping, Noël," Willie answered.

"Well, I haven't. I've come for a whole hour," Noël said, "before I lunch with Yul Brynner. I intend to enliven your poor, dreary old life by teaching you a brand new game of patience—not that childish one you play. Now, come to the table."

Obediently we sat down at the card-table.

"We need two packs—and you've got two packs," Noël said. "Splendid. Now these are the rules. The ace of spades is wild and so are the three of hearts and the eight of clubs. Right? . . . Now you deal out seven cards face down—thus." Noël dealt out the cards quickly. "Seven cards upwards, and seven cards face downwards."

Suddenly Willie turned to him. "Yer-you know, Noël," he said, "it's very ker-kind of you to invite me to stay in your chalet for three months."

Noël gazed at him in astonishment. "Now whatever crossed your strange little Chinese mind to suppose that I should issue such an invitation?" he asked. "And may I add that if ever, at some unguarded moment, such an invitation escaped my lips, it is promptly withdrawn. But what makes you imagine that I *should* ask you to stay— and for three months?"

"Wer-well, it's going to take you at least three months to teach me this patience," Willie said. "And I'd far rather learn it at *your* expense than at *mine* . . ." He paused. Then he added: "You see, my dear Noël, it may have escaped your attention—but I am in fact a thoroughly stupid man."

"Escaped my attention!" Noël exclaimed. "*What* did I say to myself when I first clapped eyes on you half a century ago? '*There*', I said to myself, 'goes a thoroughly stupid man!' And fifty years have only confirmed me in my opinion."

Willie laughed. He stretched out his hand for a moment and touched Noël's arm. "Fifty years," he said. "It's a very long time."

*   *   *

When I was staying at the Mauresque in August 1962 the house was much as usual except that, since Willie had sold his collection of Impressionist pictures, the Zoffanys were back in the living-room and in the dining-room where the Marie Laurencins had been before the war. The bookcases had been removed from the living-room which made it look cooler and lighter.

Willie greeted me warmly. He was wearing a white shirt and flowered shorts. But he *had* changed, for he looked far older than he had three months previously and the haunted expression on his face had become more pronounced. "I've had a drink already," he announced to Alan and me. "At noon I had a dry biscuit and a glass of dry wine. And I'm feeling quite benign because I'm glad to see Robin again... Incidentally, did you know that I might have had French nationality? You see, in the 1870 War France lost so many men that a decree was made by which all born in France should become French citizens. So my mother went to the British Embassy in Paris before I was born and I was born in the Embassy, so I am British."

At dinner Willie appeared in his black, double-breasted, quilted smoking-jacket with a purple design, a white shirt open at the neck, narrow black trousers and black velvet shoes with his monogram embroidered in gold braid on the toes—"a present from a fan" he told me.

He was in a reminiscent mood. "I have met all the most important people of the day," he said. "When I was young the weekend parties were terribly grand. At one of them our hostess apologised to us—I can't imagine why: 'I'm afraid I've invited Winston and Clemmie Churchill,' she said. But there weren't many bathrooms, you know. The next morning I heard from down the passage my valet saying: 'But this is Mr Maugham's bathroom.' 'Nonsense,' thundered a very aristocratic voice—'it's THE bathroom.' Country houses were like that in those days. After my mother died my father still went on building a vast house at Suresnes. You know poor Harry wrote a short book in which he chattered about the house in Suresnes among other things. But you must appreciate that our father must have been a very odd man to have built a house in the country after his wife was dead and when he must have known that there wasn't enough money for his four sons."

Willie was getting deafer than he had been three months before and his memory was failing. He suddenly announced to Alan that he intended to leave for St Moritz on Monday.

"You can't," Alan told him, "because Diana and Kim are coming to stay."

"Who are Diana and Kim?" Willie demanded. They were in fact my sister and brother-in-law, of whom he was very fond. "Who asked them? I never did. And I want to go on my travels again."

"But you've only just come back from your travels," Alan told him. "And, after all, here you've got servants to satisfy your every whim. You've got a lovely garden and a beautiful pool if you want to go for a swim. Why do you want to leave the Mauresque?"

"Because I loathe every brick of the place," Willie

replied. "I still want to travel. On my travels I've enjoyed more happiness than at any time. At first I travelled because I was of a restless nature and I enjoyed it. Then I began to travel with the idea at the back of my mind that I might find material that would be of use to me. I have always liked to see for myself the scene of action of my stories . . . Rudyard Kipling told me to go to those islands somewhere in the Far East. They weren't right for him, he said. But they were the sort of place where he thought I might pick up a story. So I went there, and I stayed for three months."

"Which was the story you got?" I asked.

"You don't just *get* a story," Willie answered. "You must know that perfectly well. You just have to wait for it to come to you. I've never written a story in my life. The story has come to me and demanded to be written."

"Where were these islands?" I asked.

"Off Australia somewhere," Willie said.

And that was as much as I could get out of him on that subject.

"My uncle at Whitstable was a cracking snob," he announced suddenly. "Do you suppose there's anything aristocratic about a clergyman?. . . But I'm getting tired and so I suppose I should be thinking of going to bed— not that I can find any consolation in sleep these days."

*   *   *

It was a warm evening and the mosquitoes seemed to be humming louder than ever. At last I managed to get to sleep. I was awoken by a ghastly noise. Someone was groaning and shrieking. I climbed out of bed and moved across to the door of my room; which I opened. Then, from along the corridor, I heard Alan get out of bed and move through the bathroom which connected his room

130

with Willie's. For the horrible sounds came from Willie's bedroom.

I had heard the sounds before, Willie was haunted.

He was very silent the following morning. Though we usually met before lunch at 12.30, drinks were never served until 12.45. We would drink one cocktail and then go into lunch, which was announced at one o'clock precisely. Sometimes Willie put me between him and Alan; sometimes he would sit at the head of the table himself.

We met again at 7.20 that evening on the terrace. Willie fidgeted with an unlit cigarette and a matchbox. "You will notice that I no longer have my sign against the Evil Eye printed on all the matchboxes," he commented. "I stopped it because so many of my guests used to pinch the matchboxes as souvenirs and I simply couldn't afford it. Your grandfather was one of the first Englishmen to travel in the south of Morocco and he ordered the sign against the Evil Eye to be inscribed on great quantities of glass he had ordered for the house in Suresnes. My father was a stranger to me when he was alive," Willie continued. "Yet somehow that sign against the Evil Eye seems to have bound us together, for as you know I've used it a great deal."

My grandfather's odd sign is printed on the jacket and stamped on the cover of all Willie's books. It was used by his American publisher as a watermark on each page of paper of his collected works. It was impressively engraved outside the gate that led into the Villa Mauresque—which Willie bought for £7,000. The sign was also over the front door of the villa. It is now my crest.

"Investigations at the British Museum," Willie told me, "suggest that the sign may possibly be intended to represent an upright sword covered by the arch of the sky.

131

It could be the symbol of a sword piercing through darkness into light. Alternatively, the vertical and horizontal lines within the arch around it may well be the cross of Lorraine. But why should my father have discovered a cross in the depths of Saharan Morocco?"

Oddly enough, I think I discovered the answer when I lived with a tribe of Tuareg while I was writing *The Slaves of Timbuktu*. The Tuareg were originally nomadic Libyans. Invasions from Carthage and Rome pressed them back into the interior. Their eyes were not accustomed to the glare of the Sahara, so they wore a veil, the *nicab*, to cover their head and forehead. Then they could not endure the thick sandstorms, so they wore another veil, the *litham*, to protect their nose and the lower part of their face. But there is evidence that the Tuareg were once Christians. Their swords are cross-hilted, the pommels of their camel-saddles take the form of a cross, and the same symbol is much used by their leather-workers and metal-workers. There are several words in the Tamachek language which suggest a Christian origin. Two striking examples are *Mesi*, meaning God, and *andjelous*, meaning angel. The names Samuel and Saul, which are rarely used by the Arabs of Africa, are common amongst the Tuareg. Roman soldiers and merchants had brought the Gospel to North Africa at the end of the first century when the Tuareg were still in Libya. Arabs who had been converted to Christianity painted the traditional symbol of strength on the walls of their houses and even drew it in the sand. Arabs and Africans—long before Islam—may well have borrowed the sign of the Cross from the Christians as a talisman to ward off the Evil Eye. The Tuareg may have taken the sign with them into the Sahara. And my uncle, Willie Maugham, the agnostic, may have been protected throughout his life by a Christian symbol without knowing it. But Willie was not in the mood to listen to any such story and besides, I was afraid it might irritate him to know that his sign was probably of Christian origin—so I said nothing.

"How much longer have we got to wait?" Willie demanded. He knew and we knew that Marius would not bring in the cocktails until 7.45. "How much longer have I got to wait, Alan?" Willie repeated.

"Two and three quarter minutes," Alan replied cheerfully.

Sure enough, the dry martinis with a sprig of mint in them arrived on time. Willie drank little wine that evening but on the terrace after dinner he ordered a peach brandy with his coffee. From the terrace we could see the distant lighthouse flickering through the trees. Willie's mind was now as intermittent as the flashes of that lighthouse. There were periods of occlusion when his mind seemed to go blank—or he would turn without reason to some new subject.

"Alan is worried as to whether I shall lose £200,000 over a contract," Willie told me, "but it won't make me any more or less important. That sum of money couldn't make me any less unhappy. And personally I don't give a fuck."

But I had an idea that he did care.

As his conversation progressed in fits and starts I was very conscious of the croaking of the frogs and the cicadas in the garden. Only three lines of telegraph wire reminded one that a road passed below the garden.

"I have learned by experience," Willie stated, "that the one sure way to rid myself of haunting memories is to set them down in black and white—to write them out of my system." He paused and turned towards Alan. "And now,

133

my dear Alan, I am very tired, so will you take me upstairs to bed?"

*　　　*　　　*

The following day Alan felt ill. The doctor was summoned, and Alan was told to remain in bed. I was therefore alone on the terrace with Willie before lunch.

"All my mistakes—all the troubles I'm in now—have been due to two things," Willie told me. "Vanity and stupidity."

"How?" I asked.

"You see, I was a quarter normal and three-quarters queer, but I tried to persuade myself it was the other way round. That was my greatest mistake. It flattered me that Syrie should throw herself at my feet. She told me that she cared for me more than anyone else in the world. And she wanted to bear my child. I was so vain and stupid I believed her . . . But she ruined my life. She made my life utter hell. You may laugh, but it's true. But it was all my own fault—because if I hadn't been vain and stupid, I'd never have listened to what she said."

Lunch was excellent. I told Annette, quite truthfully, that she looked younger than ever.

"*Il y a secret pour rester jeune—et nous le savons, nous deux,*" she said, smiling.

After lunch I went out to the pool which had been newly painted blue. The pool was kept full; water slopped gently into the garden to irrigate it and to prevent insects floating on top of the pool. An engine in a shed near by kept water flowing from the triton's mouth at the shallow end. At 4.30 I came down from the pool to find Willie looking pale and wretched outside Alan's room.

"He's not feeling too well," Willie said. "You'd better not disturb him."

134

So I wandered down into the living-room and then into the garden. Gradually the mantle of Willie's sadness descended on me. I felt defeated and lonely. I felt: if this is all that labour and suffering and fame and wealth lead up to—then what is the point of it all? At 6.15 I saw Willie sauntering along the terrace above. I called out to him and joined him.

"I don't know if you've ever walked along here," Willie said, gesturing towards the expensive lawn. "It's my favourite walk."

So along we wandered—across the shadows made by the firs and the eucalyptus trees. And I admired the view. "I used to be fond of it," Willie said. "But now the stretch means nothing to me. I just don't care for it any more."

"Why not?" I asked.

"Because I used to be able to play tennis and golf and swim, and now I can only just swim the length of the pool. And I used to have lots of friends—other writers— I've forgotten all their names—but now they're all dead or they're all gone. The place is no use to me any more. Even when we're not here it costs £2,000 a month to run and that's a lot of money... The villa now belongs to my daughter Liza—though all the contents belong to me. So I could sell all the contents and just say to her: 'Take the villa. It's yours.' And I'd like to live somewhere— perhaps in Venice—with a large living-room and two bedrooms and nothing more. I'm fed up with this place."

The conversation depressed me still further and I asked if it wasn't time for a drink. "I've had a drink already," Willie replied. "I had one at six o'clock."

"What about another?" I suggested.

"If you insist," he said, laughing suddenly.

"I do," I said. "And I'd like one too."

135

"You sit down and I'll go and get our drinks brought," Willie told me.

So off he went and minutes passed. Presently he appeared staggering under the weight of a large tray of ice and a bottle of whisky and two glasses. "There was no one about, so I did it all myself," he said triumphantly. "I even broke up the ice."

Willie measured out two large jiggers of whisky into the glasses, which he half-filled with ice. "But wait until the ice has melted a little," he told me. "Now. It's ready to be drunk," he suddenly announced.

We drank happily.

"You know, when I look back on all the stories I've published," he said, "I simply don't know how they came to be written. I really believe they just must have flowed from my pen. I can't believe that I made any effort at all. They'll be forgotten, of course, because the language they're written in will be dated."

"I bet they won't be forgotten," I said.

"I know they're translated and read all over the world because of the fan-mail I get," Willie continued. "But you must remember the intelligentsia despise me. Take that magazine that's indoors. What's it called? *Encounter*? Well, all the writers on *Encounter* despise me completely. I read it just to find out what's going on and what people are interested in. But I must confess I find it terribly boring."

Willie and I met again at 7.30; at 7.40 he asked when drinks were coming. "You'll have to wait for five whole minutes," I answered.

But, thank heavens, his mind was no longer flickering. He was aware of all that was going on. The whole evening alone with him was effortless and delightful. The secret, I thought, was not to try to fill in the gaps of

136

silence. Let him follow the direction of his own thoughts —which were totally unsentimental and totally ruthless. Of his old friend G. B. Stern, he said: "She was a vulgar Jewess. She's broke now, and I have to help her. But for thirty years she led a showy, vulgar life, flaunting her success, with two secretaries and all other kinds of nonsense. And she was so common she'd sit on the lavatory seat talking to them. That's the kind of thing she did. And did you know she wanted to marry me? Why, she'd only got to look at the mirror to know it was impossible."

Of Barbara Back he said: "She's thoroughly common and persecutes me. I see as little of her as I can. She says outrageous things about everyone, and you can't believe every word she says. She invents so much. But I've been glad to help her to the last twenty years."

"Gerald Kelly has a full-length portrait of Rosie* that he'd be delighted to show you," Willie told me later. "Also he has promised Alan a portrait of me—but he can't bear to part with it."

Willie sipped his drink reflectively. "You know, my father can't have cared a row of beans about us," he said. "But he was devoted to my mother. When she married him it was considered a terrible *mésalliance,* and all her family cut her dead. But she'd come back from India, and she must have fallen in love with him... My brother Harry stammered. He wrote a novel but I never read it. He killed himself, as you know... I'm pretty sure he was

* "Rosie" refers to Rosie Driffield, the heroine of Willie's novel *Cakes and Ale.* She is perhaps his finest female character. Rosie is also the name Willie gave to an actress with whom he had an affair for eight years, early in the century. The real Rosie was the basis for the fictional character. Her name was Ethelwyn Sylvia Jones; she was the second daughter of the dramatist Henry Arthur Jones—a contemporary of Pinero, Wilde and Shaw—who has been all but forgotten.

a queer. Charles was the best of the four of us. But he married a difficult woman I could never get on with."

I noticed that Willie's fingernails were dirty—for the very first time since I'd known him. Willie had always been extremely clean, almost immaculate. But now that was changing. At the end of the evening, outside his bedroom, he kissed me and said: "Good-night, old boy."

* * *

I had a better night because Henri has given me a flit-bomb to combat the mosquitoes. Alan is still ill with his liver complaint, but the doctor says he's improving; I said good-morning to him and then went up to the pool. At eleven Willie appeared. "Ah, there you are," he said. "No, don't get up. Just sit quiet and I'll let you know when it's time for cocktails." At 12.30 we met in Alan's room. "You're both of you late," Alan said. "It's time for cocktails." So down we went. And at 12.45 exactly Marius brought in and made a dry martini with a sprig of mint in it.

Willie began to reminisce about his family. "The Breretons came over with William the Conqueror," he told us. "One of them was beheaded by Henry VIII for being too keen on Anne Boleyn. But they'd been given land in Ireland that didn't belong to them. It belonged to the O'Neills. There was a fued. Then the Breretons invited all the O'Niells to a banquet and murdered the lot of them. They were related to Richard II and fought on both sides in the Civil War. Their last country house is now a school."

At lunch—soup and a Spanish omelette—on the table was a beautiful pale blue cloth with white embroidery. Willie observed me admiring it. "Alan and I went to a convent outside Florence where they made these cloths,"

138

he said. "I ordered the first I saw and then four more. Then Alan said: 'Hadn't you better find out how much they cost?' So I asked and when I found out I said: 'Well, we'll just have this one.' "

Suddenly Willie startled me. "Has it ever occurred to you to ask yourself what they feel about you?" he demanded.

"Who?" I asked.

"The people who are giving you this food," Willie explained. "I can tell you this, they hate the lot of us. They hate us because they find the work humiliates them."

"They may hate us as a class," I said, "but not as individuals."

"Only because I provide for their board and lodging," Willie answered.

"No," I replied. "Because they admire you as a famous writer."

"I very much doubt it. They admire the security I can give them," Willie stated. "They admire themselves for doing their jobs well. And that's all there is to it."

"I don't agree," I said. "What about the personal element?"

Thank heavens both Marius and Henri spoke only a little English.

To distract Willie I asked him if he thought there was any point in my marrying to produce an heir. "None," he said. "After all there are plenty of Viscounts already and there'll be plenty more."

"I'm glad you feel like that," I said.

"I don't even think that my work will live," Willie muttered.

I thanked him for letting me quote his line praising *November Reef* as a blurb for the novel—"I find it fresh and stirring", he had written. I felt now that Willie had accepted me as a writer, and that he no longer resented my career. "I only hope that it will help," he said. Then he asked me about the film rights and I told him how things stood.

Over coffee Willie referred again to his own work. "I'm not even sure if I'll be read in a hundred years' time," he said. "They may find me old hat . . . But I don't really care."

"All the same, when you look at those rows of books you've written . . ." I began.

"They mean nothing to me," Willie answered, fixing me with a baleful stare. "My success means nothing to me. All I can think of now are my mistakes. I can think of nothing else but my foolishness. And I've made mistakes all along the line. And the awful thing is, if I had my life to live a second time I'd make the same errors all over again. All over again."

"Has it ever occurred to you," I said—using one of his favourite expressions—"that if you hadn't made mistakes, if you'd been perfectly wise and infallible, you'd never have written as you did?"

His eyes swivelled towards me; suddenly his grim face relaxed into a smile. "You may have a point there," he admitted.

"Surely the business of the artist is to see life whole and to see it crooked," I said. "It's the writer's unique slant that gets him his audience. If you'd been a completely balanced man, sound in all your judgments, you probably wouldn't have been a success as a writer."

"And I wouldn't have had the money to make my mistakes," Willie said.

"But what were your mistakes?" I asked.

"Oh, there were so many! But Syrie was the greatest

mistake. When she came to me and when her husband cited me as co-respondent, my lawyers begged me not to marry her. They asked if I'd got twenty or thirty thousand pounds to spare and I said: 'Yes.' And they said: 'Give it to her.' And if I had done so she'd have screamed a good bit and made the hell of a fuss. But in the end she'd have accepted and married someone else. And I was saddled with her for years and she led me an unhappy existence."

After lunch Willie said we must go to make sure that Jean had been told to come round with the car. "You can never trust those servants," he said, "they always try to trick one another."

So we walked along the path that ran beside the disused tennis court and stopped outside Jean's cottage. "Jean!" Willie called out in a strong clear voice.

"*Oui, monsieur.*"

And in a moment Jean was with us. Willie told him that the car was required to take me to the airport.

"*Le Rolls ou le petit auto?*" Jean asked.

"The little car, of course," Willie replied. "Monsieur is of no consequence."

"*Mais monsieur est Viconte,*" Jean protested.

"Monsieur is of no consequence," Willie repeated firmly. "He's only my nephew."

I laughed and winked at Jean. I took Willie's arm and we walked back to the house.

*   *   *

But as I wrote these notes on the aeroplane from Nice to London, I could not help feeling relieved that I'd left the Mauresque. I felt that I was living on the edge of a volcano that might suddenly erupt. On its edge was a luxurious land, but it was a sad, sad country where happiness seldom pierced the grey clouds of melancholy. Pray God, I thought that Alan outlives poor darling Willie. Because were Alan to die first, heaven knows how Willie would manage. I believed he was suspicious now of everyone in the world with the exception of Alan and perhaps of me. But sometimes his small dark eyes swerved towards me with a flash of distrust, though he had been easier with me and sweeter to me and more open with me during this visit than he'd ever been. But it grieved me to see him so distraught by day and haunted by night. He churned over his mistakes ceaselessly, rehearsing each move, analysing each error, taking it meticulously to pieces and assembling it again to his humiliation and despair. When I looked round that desolate garden and those cold empty rooms and remembered the laughter, the excitement, and the glorious thrill so many of us felt to be alive and well and able to enjoy all the pleasures of the Mauresque in the days before the war, I felt lead in my heart. I remembered the words: *Où sont les neiges d'antan?*—where are the snows of yesteryear? Where indeed?

*   *   *

On Christmas Eve 1962, I arrived at Nice to find sweet kind Alan with a porter all at the ready, and Jean, the chauffeur, less welcoming than usual (perhaps there has been some staff trouble) but with the Rolls. The shock absorbers were even bumpier than when we were in Switzerland. On the way back Alan said I'd find Willie changed for the worse.

I found Willie in tweeds and baggy corduroys, very affable and benign. He was longing to see the photographs of the bust of his father I'd had taken for my family book. But for some reason—probably because he'd not forgiven his father for the waste of money—he was irritated that I'd driven out to see the house at Suresnes.

"Why should you want to see the house that your grandfather built in his folly? He must have known his financial condition. He must have known that he had four sons . . . I suppose he just said to himself, 'I simply don't care about them . . . Let them look after themselves . . .' But has it occurred to you that you have suffered from my father's folly? If he'd left your father a proper amount of money, your father wouldn't have been the despicable shit that he was."

At seven we met in the living-room. Willie was wearing black silk trousers, a double-breasted quilted jacket, a loose scarf and his embroidered slippers. Alan was wearing a satin waistcoat with diamond buttons and links to match. I showed Willie the photographs of the bust of his father. Alan said to Willie: "And I've seen you with your legs tucked up in that position."

At 7.30 in came cocktails—one dry martini for Willie and one for me; Alan was drinking tomato juice. Willie said that his brother Harry had written a lot about their father, but he could only remember the last sentence: "He died."

A magnificent dinner was brought by Marius and Henri. Pink Champagne was always served the first night after any guest arrived and we had oyster soup—white fondant on top; prawns with rice and curry; crêpe au rhum; cheese; dates and nuts. During dinner Willie said once again that G. B. Stern had tried to marry him, but I doubted it. Willie had no objections to his own publishers Heinemann publishing me. He is now rather deaf but benignly patient about it. He also wanted me to write a full biography of him, but I didn't think I could do it.

After dinner Willie said: "Alan and I had a friend

and I once asked him if he was the richest man in France. And he said," and Willie put his hand coyly to his mouth like a young girl, "and he said, 'Well, I'm not absolutely sure. But I suppose that I might be.' Willie paused for a moment. "Lady Bateman who's coming to lunch tomorrow did something I've always envied. She decided to visit India. And so she hired a train. A steam engine and what goes behind it; there were carriages for herself and her companion and her secretary and lady's maid and all her servants. There was a restaurant car. People can't *afford* to do that nowadays, however rich they are. One can have no idea of the luxury they lived in in those days."

The lunch party for tomorrow was discussed. "Who shall I put on my right, Alan?" Willie asked. "Lady Bateman," Alan told him. "And who shall I put on my left?" And so it went on.

Alan said: "We're having a grand lunch because it's Christmas day."

"Christmas day?" Willie said wearily. "Oh, is it really?" And went on to discuss Lord Walderon's mother's income.

*   *   *

I didn't sleep too well because the heating apparatus in the villa kept roaring and blowing, and my room became so stuffy I opened all the windows. In the morning I learned from Alan that the apparatus had gone wild and blown a hole in the wall. As it was Christmas day, no mechanic was working and nothing could be done. Later I walked with Alan to the top of the property and returned to find Willie dressed in an oddly patterned, brown and green tweed jacket with very broad lapels. At noon he was already fussing about lunch. Poor darling, he couldn't remember who was coming or where they would sit. He made three visits to the dining table to establish the *placement*. We met all the servants. Willie, Alan and I said firmly: "Happy Christmas—*Joyeux Noël*." But I'm afraid it hadn't been that so far.

"I'm bound to make a balls of it," Willie said to Alan. "You'll have to help me."

Mrs Adams and Lord Walderon arrived first. Mrs Adams was very keen on her farm in Devon and her school for delinquents. Sometimes she seemed to confuse the two. "So I put him out to stud," she said—and we weren't sure if she were talking about a prize bull or a prize deliquent. Then arrived dear Lady Bateman, aged ninety-two and looking seventy in her prime; she had got up at nine in the morning to be ready for the occasion. In the hall she shed her sables, removed a sweater and a scarf, put on a mink stole and emerged dripping with diamonds.

Willie was lost at lunch at the head of the table because Mrs Adams spoke very softly, and Lady Bateman was talking to Lord Walderon. Willie had previously flummoxed his guests by introducing me as his niece. Mrs Adams talked non-stop about her family, about animals, juvenile delinquents, vegetables, and Wellington. It was difficult to hear whether she was discussing the late Duke or a vegetable marrow.

I tried to get Willie to enter into the general conversation which ranged from Winston Churchill to the granddaughter of a duke who had run off with a lorry driver. "She met him at a roadside café," said Mrs Adams proudly. "She was *always* interested in roadside cafés."

Suddenly Willie turned on Alan inconsequentially. "What was that book I was reading by an American? For fuck's sake try to remember."

* * *

145

After we'd seen off the guests we returned to the living-room. The bright fire was the only living thing in the room. Willie, his head buried in his hands, was in complete collapse. "Take me to my room, Alan," he said. "I'm so very tired."

He was very tired and very unhappy. What shall it profit a man? ... I thought to myself. At five o'clock Willie lost his ring, so a great hunt started all over the house. I went up to search the writing-room on this jolly Christmas day. On his desk there was only one book: it's title—*Why I Am Not A Christian* by Bertrand Russell.

Alan was in tears so we rushed down to his favourite bar in Beaulieu. Alan ordered a bottle of Champagne; I had a Benedictine. Then back we went to the Mauresque so that Alan would be there when Willie woke up. "This isn't a life," Alan kept saying. "It's a nightmare I'm leading." And he was right.

I was alone with Willie for a while before dinner. He turned to me: "I don't believe in God but you do," he said to me. "Pray that I won't wake up—for that's what I hope every time I go to sleep."

God save us all.

But in the evening Willie was less sad. Indeed, over dinner—eaten at an express pace as usual—he became sweet and mellow. By this time we had all drunk a fair amount. And after dinner when he bemoaned his lot, Alan and I firmly pointed out that he had enjoyed a wonderful life on three levels: artistic, social and sexual.

"Think of the success you've had," I said. "No one has had so much so often." And I think that pleased him. For a while at least, he was—or so I felt—happy inside himself. And after Alan had put him to bed, Alan and I left in good heart to frolic happily round the bars of Villefranche.

On the following day Willie was lying on the sofa on the upper floor of the patio, going through his mail. He was delighted he had received a Christmas card from his grandsons. "As I told you, I have no objection now to you writing my biography after my death," Willie said to me. (But I wanted to do so less and less. It would have involved delving into too much unhappiness. I didn't want to turn the stones . . .).

Willie had two dry gins before lunch and became a little fuddled in the head. He kept referring to the journeys he'd made with Gerald as if he'd made them with Alan. "Alan and I are planning to sail on the *Caronia* to the Far East," he told me. "No one will ever know what a sensation I caused in the Far East . . . Alan should show you the photographs . . . The King of Johore gave a party for me, and I sat next to Edwina Mountbatten and she said: 'Willie, it is so lovely to see you again' —and three weeks later she was dead. You know, I've had the most impossible life . . . I shall never understand why all those grand people made such a fuss of me."

At that moment the two scented poodles, one beige and the other toothless and black, and George, the dachshund, came in to be given their ceremonial biscuit after meals.

At 5.30 Alan got Willie and me a whisky and left us alone, rather deliberately, I thought. So I knew I was in for a lecture. And it came. First, Willie complimented me on *The Times* review of my book on slavery. Then came the attack. "You buggered up the book through your concern with variety—and your idleness, of course. With another three or four months' work you might have written a really remarkable work. If you'd only read it through, you must have seen parts that could come out. But you had put too much of yourself into it . . . And if you're writing another book like that, don't ever say again that you were wounded in the head because nobody cares a fuck. That's not what they read you for ... *The Times* gave your last book the kind of review *The Times* seldom gives anyone. And you must have had a lot of letters as a result. But, as I said in *my* letter to you, it's going to do you no good unless you write another novel right away."

I said that as soon as I'd finished my film script, I was thinking of going to Penang.

"But why try to imitate me?" Willie asked. "Why go to the Far East when I've already written it?"

"You suggested Ceylon ..." I pointed out.

"I've written Ceylon too. But conditions are so different now that perhaps it does not matter. And you might find material for an interesting book or play ... But don't think your noble title is going to help you, because it isn't. No one will care a fuck ... In fact, if you want the truth—and I know it's depressing—you might as well know that so far as writing novels and stories is concerned, your title is a definite disadvantage ... So don't go swanking around. Try to slip away from it. Your title is a great disadvantage to you."

"Don't I know it," I said.

"You know, when I was writing I always had an idea for the next novel I wanted to write. You must have some idea. If you haven't, you'd better give up writing."

I told him briefly of two ideas I had in mind, including a novel set in Agadir.

"You're the only person to decide," Willie said. "And if you've got two ideas, then you must choose which is the more important." Then he stretched out his arms and sighed. "I know that I've been very unpleasant to you," he said. "And now I'm going upstairs to have a bath."

While I was writing these notes, Alan came in and said: "Willie was very upset, because he thought he'd been unkind to you. But it was only for your own good. There was no malice behind the attack. And of that I'm sure."

I told Alan that I realised this fully. "And I was grateful to him," I said. "My own father would never have taken the trouble to say so much to me."

*   *   *

At dinner that night Willie was in better form than he'd been since I had arrived and told us various stories. "The actress who played in *The Constant Wife* which opened in Cleveland, Ohio, gave a terrible performance and couldn't remember her lines. When I went backstage, she threw her arms round my neck and said 'I've given a ghastly performance, and I've ruined your play. But never mind. It'll run for two years.' And do you know, it did," said Willie.

Willie thought his best play was *The Circle*. He was very concerned about lunch tomorrow in Monte Carlo. "Prince Pierre puts on a lot of airs, and I won't stand for it," he announced. "I shall nod my head to him but there's no reason why you should. You're a Peer of the Realm and it would be most improper."

I said I was all for bowing if it gave anyone any pleasure. After all, it didn't hurt me. "I dare say," said Willie, "but everyone else will be watching you. And I don't want you to do it."

Willie was reading a book in French about Henry III. "At the present moment he's my favourite French king," he told me. "He was queer, of course. But I must tell you that the whole lot of them at that time were a thoroughly bad lot—murdering each other constantly and, mark you, they were a crowd of scallywags."

Since I'd been there I'd felt quite deliciously sleepy—as if I'd been doped. Why should that be? Did Annette pop some drug into her delicious cooking? I felt gloriously tired, and I was delighted to be in bed before ten o'clock and alone. But I slept badly. I felt that the Villa Mauresque was haunted. And I could not help remembering constantly that tortured old man in the bedroom along the corridor.

*   *   *

At eleven a.m. I found Willie pacing the living-room. "You may wonder why you find me walking up and down this room," he said. "You find me walking up and down because I've nothing on earth else to do."

Earlier I'd strolled round the garden with Alan who dreaded my departure because he'd be all alone with Willie again. Then Alan said, "Why don't you go in and talk to Willie?" But the trouble was that so often now when I was alone with him, I got tongue-tied. I dredged deep in my mind to fish up a story, but if it was at all long or at all complicated I knew I wouldn't pierce through the barrier of his deafness. So my only hope was that he'd do the talking.

All we could manage was a little small talk about Riviera personalities, and then silence fell. "It's lovely to look through the window and see oranges growing on a tree," I said idiotically. Willie turned and stared out of the window. "I suppose it is," he said. "I hadn't really noticed it."

There was silence again. Willie could no longer look out of the window. He was imprisoned tight in the web of his haunting past. There was so much I'd have liked to ask him—so much I'd have loved to find out about.

*　　*　　*

The car had been ordered for 12.30 to take us to lunch in Monte Carlo. "Your hostess at lunch today has been married four times," Willie told me, in his characteristically slanderous way, "and so far as we know, during her whole life she has only enjoyed nine months of married bliss. Don't ask me how she got rid of her four husbands —because I don't know. My friend Lady Bateman will also be there . . . She's immensely rich and very kind, but a tremendous snob."

On Willie's instructions the three of us had put on our best suits. At 12.25 Willie had begun to fidget and to ask if it were not time to leave. The minutes dragged by. At last we walked out of the dark brown room—dark brown silk on the sofas, dark brown high-backed chairs, mainly dark brown Aubusson carpet—into the glorious sunshine pouring from a bright blue sky.

"Did I tell you how I came to buy this Rolls?" Willie asked me.

"No," I said.

"Well, when I was a dramatist I wrote a play . . ."

"No, you wrote a novel," Alan corrected.

"That's right, Alan. A novel called . . . What *was* it called, Alan?"

"*Theatre.*"

"*Theatre*," said Willie, "that's it. And some French dramatist . . ."

"Souvajon," said Alan.

"Souvajon made a play from it. And the critics were a bit sniffy about it. But every actress wanted to play it. And it was done all over Europe, time and time again.

151

And with the royalties I got from it I bought this car . . .
And Alan and I have travelled quite long journeys in
Europe. And it's never given any trouble—though it's
now five years old."

"Ten," said Alan.

"What's that?" Willie asked.

"It's ten years old," Alan said.

"Is it really?" Willie muttered. "I had no idea."

When we passed the yacht harbour, Alan said that
there were two big yachts in, owned by Greeks. "One
of them's very rich," Willie said, "and we must be nice to
him, because he's got a very large yacht. The only thing
wrong with him is that he's a crashing bore."

"What time would you like the car to come to take
you back?" Alan asked.

Willie's face had now set into grim lines of displeasure.
"As soon as we arrive," he snapped.

Alan gave me a worried look. Willie nearing ninety
was unpredictable. Anything could happen from one
moment to the next. And it was Alan—untiring, loyal,
patient Alan—who had to cope. I honestly believe that
had it not been for Alan's unceasing care and devotion
during the last years of Willie's life, my uncle would have
gone mad or killed himself.

"Millicent is an old friend of yours," Alan said. "And
she's giving a little lunch-party in your honour. She'll be
very disappointed if you don't come."

"Then she'll have to be disappointed, won't she?"
Willie replied.

But when the car drew up outside the block of flats
behind the Promenade des Anglais, we managed to persuade Willie to get out of the car. We were met by a
servant who led us through a series of dark marble patios
to an extremely small lift. Our hostess was sitting on the

landing outside her flat to greet us as we stepped out of the lift door.

"Willie!" she cried. "Welcome, darling!"

And she gave him a smacking kiss on both cheeks. For a moment Willie did not move. He stared at her in silent distaste. Then he spoke: "There's only one excuse for plump women like you," he said, "and that is that they should have no clothes on."

"Oh, you're so witty, Willie!" Millicent tittered a trifle nervously.

"No, I'm not," Willie replied. "I'm perfectly serious. Take off all your clothes. I want to see what you've got."

Millicent gave a strained laugh and turned to us. "Isn't he witty!" she exclaimed once again.

"If you don't take your clothes off, I shan't come to lunch," Willie said firmly.

Millicent's smile froze and she fixed her faded eyes on Alan in appeal for help. As usual Alan saved the situation, and a few moments later, while we were being introduced to Millicent's guests, Willie was his usual courteous self.

"I refer to you throughout the Riviera as my fiancé," Millicent announced to me. "Because your uncle said I ought to marry you."

I said it was a delightful Christmas present and came to me as a delicious surprise.

"So I've put you at the head of the table," Millicent told me. "Because I thought you ought to get used to glowering at me across the table when the food isn't too good."

"Splendid," I said. "I'll glower."

"You know, I change as soon as I marry a man," Millicent warned me. "Before I've married him I press him to drinks. 'Have another tot, sweetie pie,' I say. But as soon as I'm married to the man I say, 'What? Do you want another drink, you drunken sot!'"

From then on I knew lunch would be fun—and it was. Marion Bateman appeared in sables with a sapphire toque to match her sapphire rings. Apparently her maid brushed cornflower into her hair one and a half hours a day to keep it "shining blue".

Willie got a little restless as we waited for His Serene Highness the Prince de Polignol, who was treated as a crowned head in Monaco. And presently everyone rose, and into the room there walked a slim elegant weary man with a short clipped white moustache and a grey face close to death, I thought, dressed in a pearl grey suit and very white linen. The women curtsied low. And the men bowed. And so did I. If it gave the poor old thing any pleasure, why shouldn't I?

The food and wine were magnificent; turbot and Liebfraumilch, baby lamb and Burgundy, crêpes and Champagne.

Alan was nervous that Willie who was sitting opposite the Prince would say something rude, but he was at his most benign and was amused by Millicent treating me as her fiancé. "My congratulations," said the Prince when we left.

*   *   *

In the car Willie said: "You've made the lunch party. You were gay and kept the conversation going. And that was just what was wanted. It's all amusing to you. But Alan and I see the same people day in and day out. And it's hard to think of anything to say to them. And Prince Pierre irritates one because of the grand manners he puts on. Who gives a fuck about royalty these days? And he

154

isn't royalty anyhow. And I'm afraid he's going to die at any moment. And he knows it."

* * *

I left the Mauresque on the following morning. Willie said good-bye to me very sweetly and said he wished that I'd stayed longer. On the way to the airport—where I was writing these notes, the plane having been delayed an hour—Alan tried to persuade me to write a *full* biography of Willie. "You're the only person who can do it," he kept saying. "You're the only person who knows . . . and you're the only person that I'll tell the *whole* story to . . . Posterity are going to want a full picture of him—not just the nice things. They'll want to see the whole man. For instance, who else knows *all* about Syrie and Gerald? . . . You know, Willie never really liked sleeping with women. He slept with Rosie who was the daughter of a dramatist and married into the peerage. But then Beerbohm Tree wrecked it all one night at supper at the Savoy by telling Rosie in front of Willie that she didn't stand a chance with Willie because Willie was a queer. Tree was jealous. And that finished it."

I told Alan that I didn't want to write a full-length book about Willie in which I'd have to go into every detail.

* * *

I next stayed at the Mauresque in November 1963. As usual, Alan and Jean met me at the airport. My aeroplane was late; so by the time we reached the villa Willie had gone upstairs for his siesta. We met for tea at four. "From my window I saw you striding through the garden as if you had a whole army of soldiers

155

following you," Willie said. "Are you bursting with excitement and money?"

"Excitement, yes; money, no," I answered.

"At least you don't deceive yourself as most English people do," Willie observed. "If people in England think the Germans are fond of them, they are making a great mistake. The Germans are getting very rich and very powerful. There's only one thing they really want—to win the next war. They are now as proud and arrogant as ever."

Willie was sitting in an armchair at the far end of the long living-room because the light was better for his eyes. He was wearing an old tweed coat, a blue shirt open at the neck, a red scarf, baggy crumpled grey flannel trousers and worn suede shoes. "I've been reading a book by a woman writer called Agatha Christie," he said. "Have you ever heard of her, Robin? . . . Did I tell you that Alan and I went to Portugal, and the General— what's his name?—Salazar, said we ought to meet some of the aristocracy. So they came to collect us in a great limousine with armoured cars in front of us and behind of us and lots of motorcycle outriders, and they drove us out to the country, and we met all the aristocracy at a big lunch. Then they asked us to a grand dinner. But I lied and said I couldn't accept because I was dining with some authors. At 8.30 or nine, Alan and I went into the dining-room of our hotel and sat down to a quiet meal alone together. At that moment the double doors were flung open, and General Salazar's A.D.C. came in followed by a bevy of important ladies who wanted me to sign copies of books of mine they'd got. But of course I'd been caught out in a monstrous lie because they could see I wasn't at dinner with a lot of authors. So I did the only thing I could under the circumstances. I signed the books; I did nothing else whatsoever . . .

"Then we were invited to the wine-making on the Douro. I was given six bottles of port. So when your father came to stay here, I opened a bottle. 'It's quite nice wine,' your father said, 'but it's not port.' I was furious," Willie said, chuckling. " 'But I brought it back myself from Portugal,' I said, 'I *know* it's port.' However, as you know, your sainted father always thought he knew best. 'I've been buying port now for Lincoln's Inn for over fifty years,' he told me, 'I *know* port and I can tell you with complete authority *this isn't port*.' I was enraged," Willie said, laughing, "but I had to give up trying to convince him . . . Your father was a horrible man, but he was brilliant. He was beastly to your mother —you probably don't know about that, but I do . . . and I've heard from everyone who had anything to do with him that he was utterly hateful. The trouble was that he didn't like the human race; he'd got no patience with fools. And as we know, most human beings *are* fools. He was quite an odious man. Charlie was the nicest one of us . . . By the way, who is Harold Nicolson?"

I told Willie, although I was aware of course that he knew—but I had to speak very loudly because he was now getting very deaf.

"I'm a very insignificant person," Willie announced, "and my opinion is of no consequence. But how do you get to Greece?"

"Flap your wings," said Alan, and Willie smiled. He was in an extremely affable mood.

"At lunch tomorrow there'll be some princess or other eating with us," Willie said. "And you know, she'll be very glad to come because, as I've discovered during my long life, royalty are always every happy to get a free meal."

I laughed.

"No, I mean it," Willie insisted. "You see, most of them are terribly hard up. They really need food."

"Tell me, Willie," Alan said, "you must make the decision. Shall I try to make an effort and stop eating so much—or shall I let myself go and just let my face go to pot?"

"Well," Willie said, "I wouldn't like to make my comment, Alan. But if you insist, then I must admit that I would have said that your face has gone to pot already. And since I'm so much more attractive than you are, I cannot imagine why it should be you that has all the success."

Willie and Alan were both genuinely devoted to each other but Alan—especially on travels—had a terrible time of it. He adored Willie, but he found it hard only to be able to get away for half an hour a day.

Willie's affable mood continued. One day we drove into Monte Carlo for a lunch party. We entered the Hotel de Paris and Willie walked straight forward. Alan said gently: "No, Willie, to the right." Willie turned right and was confronted by a very long grand piano. "But I don't *want* to play the piano, Alan," he said. "There's no point to it. You'll never persuade me to play it. I refuse to. I haven't brought my music. But I do want a Bible. A Bible with very large type, so I can read it."

"Why do you want a Bible particularly?" I asked.

"I don't really want a Bible so much as an Old Testament," Willie replied. "I want to read the story about that king—what was his name?—Saul. And about his son Jonathan and about David. I'm quite sure that if you really think about it the whole thing was a completely queer affair, I'd like to read about it again."

*　　*　　*

When I went downstairs the following morning I could see that Willie was in a bad mood and suffering from his eyes. The curtains had been partly drawn in the over-heated room in which he was sitting with Alan at the card-table, playing patience. Outside, the terrace was dappled with green shadows, and the cypresses reached for the open sky, and the eucalyptus trees were still and quite immobile in the wonder of the balmy day. But Willie would not go outside.

"He's in a strange mood today," Alan said.

The day dragged on in half darkness. The sun was now finding a way between the cypresses to warm the terrace. I felt very claustrophobic. Willie's eyes were definitely failing. Slight cataracts were forming and he could not read for as long as he used to. Occasionally he would belch and fart.

That morning Alan entertained me with stories and facts about Willie. "Eighty million copies of his books have been sold," he told me. "He's written one hundred and twenty-two short stories and of these about eighty have been performed on television. All his books and short stories are being reprinted in America. Penguin have produced over one hundred thousand copies of nine or ten of his books. Plays of his are being performed all over the world. He's written twenty-six altogether."

Alan's stories about Willie were splendid. On a recent journey, Alan had left Willie on the platform by a book-stall while he went off to see about their luggage. When he returned Willie had disappeared. After a few minutes of frantic search Alan found my uncle deep in conversation with two British tourists, a married couple from Sheffield. The wife led Alan discreetly aside.

"What a nice old gentleman," she said. "He was such a duck that we had to ask him his name. And you'll never guess what he said. Do you know—the poor old soul—he thinks he's Somerset Maugham."

But sometimes Willie *was* recognised. He was in the lift in a hotel in which he and Alan were staying when a woman approached him and said: "You're Mr Somerset Maugham. I recognise you from your photographs." Willie thought he would be gay and facetious. "I'm sorry to hear that," he said, "because I consider myself so much better looking than my photographs."

"Oh no, you're not," the woman replied firmly. "Indeed you're not."

*   *   *

I was the only guest at the Villa Mauresque for the weekend of Willie's ninetieth birthday—on January 25th, 1964. Telegrams, letters and presents flowed in from all corners of the world. The villa was besieged by reporters and cameramen. "I really don't know what they're making all this fuss about," Willie said. "They can't seriously think it's important. It's all extremely tiresome."

"Never mind," Alan said cheerfully, "your next important birthday won't be until you are a hundred."

"I don't suppose I shall live that long," Willie said firmly.

"In Nice there's a pensioner who's one hundred and four," Alan said. "They say he's quite spry."

"One hundred and four," Willie exclaimed. "No! I definitely refuse to live to one hundred and four. I don't like the sound of it at all. Fer-fuck one hundred and four."

*   *   *

On the Friday before his birthday I had slept badly and awoken late. At noon Henri came in and said would

I please dress quickly because monsieur was drinking cocktails.

"At noon?" I asked in surprise.

"Monsieur's hours are rather irregular," Henri explained.

I dressed and hurried downstairs. I found Willie in the living-room drinking a martini. He scowled as I approached. "Where have you sprung from?" he asked.

"Bed," I told him.

"Well, I hope you don't expect any food," Willie said. "There isn't enough, and I don't see why Alan and I should go short of food merely because you've arrived. I can't imagine why you've arrived anyhow."

"Because you asked me to stay," I answered. Then I tried to cheer him up. "They're doing *The Circle* on ITV," I told him. "*Home and Beauty* is playing at the Ashcroft, there are eulogies on the BBC, and one hundred and sixty bookshops have full displays—all in honour of your birthday."

"They can go fuck themselves for all I care," Willie said.

"Already over four hundred letters of congratulation have arrived," I told him.

"I don't know why they should be so stupid," Willie replied.

"Well, at least they took the trouble to write," Alan pointed out. "They bought paper, an envelope and a stamp."

"I still think it's stupid of them," Willie said. "And I don't care."

But I think in a way he did care. A telegram arrived from Prince Pierre of Monaco. "The Queen of England is a sensible person," Willie proclaimed. "She's a strong-minded woman who knows her own mind. You won't find *her* sending me a telegram."

*   *   *

The telephone never stopped ringing. We were telephoned by the *Daily Express*, the *Daily Mail*, *Time* and *Life*, the *Herald*, the *Sunday Telegraph*, the *Daily Mirror*. In the evening Willie was in a better mood. He now admitted that he was pleased by the four hundred letters and the one hundred cables and telephone calls from all over the world. He was delighted to get a charming letter from the Duc de Nemours—"Do you realise," he said to me, "that if they hadn't done away with it in France, he would be the king?" He was amused by cables from the Poet Laureate, John Masefield; from Nancy Mitford, and from the skipper and crew of the trawler *Somerset Maugham*, based on Hull. He was touched by Bob Boothby's telegram. He was now pleased with the presents—the plant from the Mayor of Cap Ferrat, the handkerchiefs from a lady admirer in America with his signature embroidered on each one, the shawl, the pocket book, the scarves and so on. "It's very kind of them to make so much fuss," he said.

Willie enjoyed his dinner of oyster soup, *canard à l'orange*, soft cheese, crystallised fruit, Champagne, peach brandy. Alan told him that before dinner we had been amusing ourselves by talking about all the disreputable things we had done in the past.

"I'm sure both your pasts were disreputable," Willie said, "but I can't imagine it was any fun."

"Oh, Willie!" Alan said. "Think of your own past. Didn't you have fun? You had more fun than any of us."

"I doubt it," Willie answered. "I doubt if I had half as much."

162

So Alan and I reminded him of various episodes in his life when he did have great fun. Willie listened with a smile. "And now I'm very tired," he said. "You must help me up the stairs to bed."

*   *   *

On the morning of his birthday I found Willie lying in bed. The photograph of his mother who had been dead for eighty years looked down upon him from the bedside table on which it always stood. Around Willie's shoulders was wrapped a thick pillar-box-red shawl. The quilt over his bed was covered with cables—many of them unopened. Willie was desultorily reading Racine's *Britannicus*.

"Happy birthday, Willie," I said.

He looked up grimly. "What was that?" he asked.

"Happy birthday," I replied, speaking louder. "Here is your present." And I handed him the Nonesuch edition of the Bible in three volumes with large clear print which he could read. At that stage, throughout the first hours of the morning, Willie's mood was good. But he obviously wasn't feeling well, for his face was drawn. A black fog seemed intermittently to envelop his mind. Cables and letters continued to pour in, but he now took no notice of them except that now and again he would scowl at a particular greeting when he opened it. At eleven, Alan and I left him for a while, begged half a bottle of Champagne from Marius, wrapped it in a copy of *The Times* and walked to the end of the garden to avoid the press —past lovely blue spernum, mimosa trees, arum lilies, heliotrope in bloom and trees of tangerines. We drank the Champagne and then went back to Willie. He had discarded the shawl and Racine. "I don't know how the actors of the day ever *spoke* those long speeches of his—

163

or how the audience endured them," he said. "They go on for pages and pages."

By this time he was toying with the Old Testament. "It's very good print," he told me. "I can read it." He opened a volume at the first Book of Samuel and read the passages about Saul and David and Jonathan. "There's no doubt about it," he said. "They were all in love. It was a queer set-up, if ever I knew one. No one reading the story can but be certain of their relationship —the three of them. But I wonder what the priests make of it—after all they have to study it almost every day. Surely even *they* can't have any doubt about what it was all about. Now you must go because I'm feeling rather tired."

Unfortunately, a few minutes later, the doctor arrived on the patio.

"My uncle's feeling rather tired," I warned him.

"So will *you* when you're ninety," the doctor replied, and walked towards Willie's bedroom. "You'd better come with me," he said.

When we entered the bedroom, Willie was sitting in an armchair. "I'm putting on my new suit in honour of my birthday," he told me. Then he noticed the doctor. "I thought that no photographers were allowed," he said. "Get all that nonsense over with. Why have you come here?"

"I'm your doctor."

"Then don't try to give me your usual stuff, I know you're trying to poison me."

However, presently Willie calmed down and I left him alone with the doctor. I wandered out into the garden. When I returned to the house I found Willie dressed and with his overcoat on. He was evidently now in an extremely bad mood. His mouth was pursed. His lips seemed almost to join his nose. He was in a silent white rage, radiating anger. The Rolls was outside.

"Thank Jean for the flowers," Alan said to Willie. He muttered a few words.

"As you know, monsieur," Jean said, "it only happens once a year."

We were silent as the Rolls clattered and bumped its way over the Moyenne Corniche to Monaco. As we approached a new block of flats Alan asked: "What time would you like to be taken back?"

"As soon as we arrive," Willie replied, as he had done before.

I was afraid we were going to have the usual scene. A group of photographers was waiting outside the entrance to the block of flats. The Rolls stopped. I was nearest to the kerb and Jean opened the door for me to get out. At that moment Willie spoke again: "I'm staying here," he informed us. "I have no intention of leaving the car."

By then I'd got out of the car. The television cameramen, photographers and journalists were advancing.

"Would you like to drive off?" Alan asked Willie.

"No," Willie replied. "I'm quite happy where I am."

By this time the car was surrounded. Cameras were pressed against the windows. "Are the photographers bothering you, Willie?" I asked.

"No," Willie answered. "I don't see any of them. But I don't want to go in and meet all these people." Willie beckoned to me and I leant into the car. "Where are we?" he asked.

I explained that we were going to a lunch party in his honour. "Well, no one ever told me," Willie complained.

"Yes they did," Alan said. "Many times."

"Willie, please get out," I said. "It's the easiest solution."

"I won't move," Willie answered. "If that whole gang of people think I'm going to lunch with them, they're very mistaken."

"You go inside," Alan said to me. "Explain that we'll be up in ten minutes."

Sure enough, ten minutes later Willie entered the crowded room, followed by Alan. He looked pallid and grim. At first he refused to greet anyone but presently he relaxed and spoke a few words. Once we had sat down to lunch he was less angry but then, to our horror, at the end of the excellent meal there entered press and television cameramen. Willie was dragged to his feet and with an effort blew out the single candle on his cake.

After the cameramen had departed, the lady sitting at Willie's left turned to him and said: "I'm told there's a pensioner in Nice who's still alive and kicking at one hundred and four."

Willie glared at her. "Fer-fer-fer-fuck one hundred and four," he said. There was an embarrassing pause.

Soon afterwards we left and drove back in grim silence to the Mauresque. Alan had already cancelled our invitation to a dinner party in Willie's honour. As we moved towards the door of the villa I took Willie's arm. Suddenly he turned on me in a rage. "Why do you do that?" he asked me furiously. "Can't you see how much it annoys me?"

The rest of the day passed in sadness.

*　　*　　*

My diary, written late that night, ended with the words. *'Oh, dear God, let me not live to ninety.'*

*　　*　　*

166

The following morning Alan told me that Willie was so tired he would spend the whole day in bed. But Willie was shuffling round the corridors at ten o'clock in the morning, muttering to himself. Before lunch he seemed to have rallied.

"Alan and I saw Sir John Moore's tomb at Corunna," Willie announced over cocktails, "and the famous poem is engraved on it. And it made me cry ... We saw him killed, you know."

"No, Willie," Alan said, "but we saw his tomb."

However, I do believe that in his imagination, Willie *did* see Sir John Moore killed.

"What date did he die?" I asked.

"1780," Alan replied.

"At that period you were quite a sweet young thing," Willie said to him.

"Do you see how cruel he is to me!" Alan exclaimed, laughing.

"Did I tell you the story of the Spaniard who cooked for his wife?" Willie asked me.

"No."

"Well, he prepared a special dish for her lunch one day," Willie said. " 'Did you like that dish?' he asked her after she had finished eating. 'Yes,' she replied enthusiastically. 'It was your lover's liver,' he told her." Willie paused for a moment. "I've always found that a pretty little tale ... But then people tell me my taste in stories is slightly peculiar."

*   *   *

When I arived at the Villa Mauresque in June 1964 Willie's mind had more periods of occlusion than ever. He had grown very suspicious and accused all the servants of stealing his money.

"You know, the world, during my life, has somehow been involved with me," he said that night at dinner, "and somehow—I don't quite know how—I have been involved with the world. But I can tell you this . . . I am one of the most horrible old men alive today. I've been so wicked," he cried suddenly. "I've been so cruel."

The following evening I stayed alone with Willie so that Alan could have an evening out for once. Alan left at 6.15. All seemed well. I sat with Willie in the living-room. Cocktails arrived punctually at seven o'clock.

"Shall we go out on to the terrace for our drinks?" Willie asked.

"Yes, please."

The cocktails were put on a table on the terrace. Willie gazed around him. "You know," he said, "after I die, all this will be taken away from me—the whole property, every square foot of it, and all the furniture and all the pictures. I shan't even be able to take a single table with me. They'll take the whole lot and I shall have nothing at all left." He paused and gazed at me through his watery slit-eyes. "It's not a good prospect to look forward to," he added.

After he'd finished his drink, Willie asked what time it was. I told him it was 7.23.

"Good," Willie said. "We've only seven minutes to wait."

On the dot of 7.30, Marius announced supper and in we went to the dining-room. We drank half a bottle of Champagne. Dinner was excellent. Willie's appetite was still good and he was in better spirits.

"I wrote," he told me, "because there were things I felt obliged to say. I can't remember a single novel now. It's all so very long ago . . . I don't think I was a great writer—I can't remember."

After dinner we sat in the living-room. Willie began to get worried. "What time is it?" he asked.

"About nine."

"Where is Alan?"

"As you know, he's gone out for a while."

Willie was silent for a moment. "I have a question to ask you," he said presently. "What time is it? What time is it?"

"Five past nine."

"And where is Alan?"

"Out."

Willie was silent. I picked up *Country Life* and began to read. Willie trembled as he turned his face towards me. "What time is it?" he asked.

"Ten past nine."

"Where is Alan?"

"He's gone out," I answered.

There was another heavy silence. Then Willie turned on me. His hands clawed frantically at the air. "I know you are the stupidest member of your family," he said, "but perhaps you can answer a simple question. What time is it?"

"Half past nine."

"Where is Alan?"

"I don't know."

"You don't know what town he's in?"

"No, I don't. Probably Nice."

Willie glowered at me, lit a cigarette with trembling hands and began to smoke furiously. As I looked wretchedly through *Country Life* I tried to make myself think what house I would buy if I had any money in the world and any leisure. Suddenly Willie turned on me again. "Perhaps you would be good enough to answer me another question," he said acidly.

169

"Certainly."

He stood up and once again his hands clutched the empty air above his head. "What arrangements have you made with Alan?" he asked.

"None."

"Where has he gone?" Willie now addressed me as if I were a complete stranger. "When will Mr Searle be back?" he demanded.

"I don't know."

"You must know."

"I'm sorry, but I don't."

"Then I shall wait here until Mr Searle *does* return," Willie announced. And down he sat and began to smoke through his cigarette holder. His face was grim and his tiny eyes were glittering. Suddenly he turned on me once more. His face was contorted with hatred. "Where do you live?" he asked, in a voice quivering with rage.

"In Brighton."

"Don't be wilfully stupid," he said. "I mean where are you staying tonight?"

"Here in your villa," I replied firmly. "I'm your guest."

"No, you're not," he answered. "There's no room for you. Who are you? What room do you think you are going to sleep in?"

Abruptly he stood up and tottered out of the room. I could hear him screaming at the staff in the kitchen. I continued to read *Country Life*. Willie came back into the room. "Where is Alan?" he demanded. "I'm asking you, when is he coming back? When will Mr Searle be here? What are you doing in this house? What is your name?" Out he rushed once more and came back—this time with Marie, Annette's assistant in the kitchen.

"Dans quelle chambre est-ce que monsieur va se coucher?"

170

"Mais en haut, monsieur," Marie answered.

"Dans quelle chambre?" Willie demanded.

"Dans la chambre à lui."

"Montrez la moi."

So upstairs we trooped. Marie, terrified, opened the door of my bedroom. Willie glared into the empty room. Then he flicked the lightswitch. "These lights will be turned out in five minutes," he told me. "I'm not going to pay for any more electricity for you than that."

I felt I must try to say something pleasant. "Goodnight, Willie," I said. "Thank you very much for an excellent dinner."

Willie tottered towards me, shaking with rage. I thought he would strike me. "That's the very least you should say to me," he shouted. "I expect more than that." And he shuffled angrily from the room.

Marie, in tears, gave me a look of commiseration before she left. Willie slammed the bedroom door shut. I could hear him screaming and shouting along the patio.

Alan returned at about 10.30. Presently he came up to see me. "The staff are in tears," he reported. "I haven't had an evening out for a whole year, and now I shall feel I can never go out again." Then he left to cope with Willie once more. His devotion was marvellous —but I was afraid he must now lead a wretched life.

"I'm sure that if Willie had a knife or gun he would have killed me," the entry in my diary for that day concludes. *"He is, I'm now convinced, a maniac. It is his quality of malignancy that pierces me with fear.*

"God save us all."

* * *

The next morning Willie had completely forgotten his fit of lunacy but I think he was left with the vague impression that he had been unpleasant to me and felt that he should make amends for it. When I came out of my room on the way to the pool he was lying asleep on the patio. He awoke and greeted me affectionately. "You're looking very smart," he said. In fact I was wearing an ordinary white towelling dressing-gown which belonged to the Mauresque and which hung behind the door of my bedroom. Later he appeared at the pool. "You know, I've slept all morning," he said. "I don't know what I've been working myself up about . . . But I've been trying to sleep my life away . . . You must realise that it was all right for Jesus Christ, every bit of it. He could arrange things just as he wanted them. But my problem is that I simply can't. That's the whole difference between the two of us. And I am tired—so dreadfully tired. And I don't really know anything, and I find it very humiliating. But I don't really care a fer-fuck. Is it morning or afternoon?"

"Morning."

"I hoped it was afternoon . . . But presently Alan will make us a cocktail, and if it's Sunday morning, then perhaps we could have a second cocktail."

We drank two cocktails; then we went in to lunch and ate Spanish omelette, macaroni with a cheese sauce, and cherries; we drank a delicious white Macon. After his siesta Willie came out on to the terrace again, but his mind was now wandering. "I'd like a drink," he told me, "and then I'd like lunch."

"But you've already had lunch," I said.

"No, I haven't," he replied. "I haven't had any lunch. And I'm thirsty and hungry and miserable. And I'm not Jesus Christ—because he could do things that I can't. And the whole business of life was infinitely more simple for him than it is for me."

"Would you like a biscuit?" I asked.

"I don't *want* a biscuit," he said. "I just want my lunch."

However, Alan produced a sandwich and all was well.

*   *   *

The following day we drove into Monte Carlo to lunch with Willie's old friend Lady Bateman. Willie was in a dangerous mood. "This is a very indifferent meal," he told his hostess who beamed at him politely because she hadn't heard a word he had said. We were drinking Champagne. Willie suddenly said: "I'd like a whisky or something to drink. I don't ask for much. As a thoroughly second-rate writer there's nothing very much I deserve. But if I hadn't had a stammer I could have been a great man. And when I went to Russia in 1917 the whole history of the world might have been different."

At that moment we were served with asparagus.

"I wrote a story about asparagus," Willie said. "I cannot remember now what I called it. But it's been published all over the world in every single language." Then he looked at Lady Bateman with an expression of hatred. "And can you tell me *why*?" he demanded. "Why, whenever people eat asparagus they bring up that story? Why should I write a story for fools all over the world to read?"

"I do so agree," Lady Bateman said, but she had no idea what he was talking about.

*   *   *

The days of my visit dragged by. Willie was at his most irritable in the morning. He would sit like a malignant crab on the first-floor gallery above the patio. To leave my room, I had to pass by him.

"Good-morning," I said to him loudly and cheerfully as I approached. He scowled and pursed his lips. Loathing slanted from his half-closed eyes. "Good-morning *and*?" he asked. The sun was shining from a clear blue sky. "It's a wonderful morning," I said tritely.

"And so you're idling as usual." The angry words seemed to slither from his mouth.

"No," I said, patting the film script I carried tucked under my arm. "I'm taking some work up to the pool with me."

Willie grunted unpleasantly. I left him. When he was in these moods I could almost believe that at some stage in his career Willie had made a compact with the Devil. "If you make me the most successful writer," Willie might have said to him, "you can have my soul." And now the Devil has come to claim his property. He proved his ownership daily.

We now had cocktails on the terrace at noon because the meal-times have been advanced an hour so that Willie could feel that he was getting through the day quicker.

"You can't marry anyone unless you've got something to offer," Willie said to me. "And *you've* got nothing at all. Nothing. And I wish I knew where Tahiti was. But I'm ignorant about these things. It must have arrived out of the sea somehow."

After lunch, on the way out of the living-room into the garden, Willie stopped at the top of the steps. Once again he looked round the garden. "You may think that all this belongs to me," he said. "But it doesn't. It belongs to someone else. When I die it will all be taken away from me. And I shan't have anything left." He leaned

174

his head against the white-washed wall and burst into tears. "I'm so old and so tired," he sobbed. "Why can't they let me die? Why can't they? I'm so miserable. I want to die so much."

His grief was heart-rending. I felt the tears scudding into my eyes. It was anguish to see a person one has once respected and loved suffering such despair. But the sad truth was Willie was still afraid of death. Coffee came; I gave Willie a match for his cigarette. Presently he was composed and talking to Alan about visiting Tahiti.

*　　*　　*

In the last year of Willie's life I visited the Mauresque twice—but I will not dwell on his fits of rage and misery.

Willie was now very old and very frail. But at times he now began to dwell more on the happier side of his past and tell stories about the kings, queens and princesses he had known and the splendours of his life.

"You know," Willie suddenly said, "before the war the King of Sweden came here to lunch. I had previously asked what His Majesty would like to eat. The answer was 'Roast beef'. So my cook Annette prepared a succulent dish of roast beef for the king. It was served to him, and he began to eat it with relish. Suddenly there was a terrible clatter from where the king was sitting. All conversation stopped. Everyone thought the king had flung down his knife and fork to demand silence for the story he was telling.

"Then we all saw that his false teeth—both the top set and the bottom—had fallen on to his plate. But the king remained perfectly calm. He continued talking—though somewhat less articulately. Then he polished his false teeth with his napkin, popped them back into his mouth, and finished his story. You see," Willie exclaimed, "he was a real gentleman."

However, later in the day he might grow tired and depressed again and Alan and I would try to cheer him up. "It must mean something to you to be so well known," I said to him.

Willie smiled. "But you know, London is well known. I'm sure there must be scores of people in the world who have heard of London and haven't heard of me ... I must tell you that the cathedrals haven't been very kind to me lately. They are so very tall and so very imposing."

I presumed Willie was referring to some of the royal personages he had met in the past.

"But you know," Willie continued. "I don't care any more. It all doesn't amount to anything. No one in the world cares about me any more."

"Nonsense," I said.

"It's true, you know," Willie persisted. "I'm quite forgotten. No one thinks about me or cares about me— not a row of beans. And anyhow, kings, queens and princesses—the whole bloody royalty—they don't really amount to anything. I led a very grand life in the days of my success. But it didn't last for long. I used to drink with kings and queens. But I can't remember their names. I have to speak very quickly these days because no sooner have I opened my mouth than the matter flies from my mind."

I handed him a cigarette and lit it for him. "That's extremely kind of you," he said. "You know, I've always wondered how it would be to have a relationship with someone who had lived two or three thousand years before you. Even if it were a brief relationship. Speaking of relationships—do you know my nephew Robin? He's

176

a very pleasant person. He's promised to visit me. I wonder if on your travels you ever met him?"

"I am Robin," I said.

"No," Willie replied.

"I am Robin Maugham."

"That is as it may be. But the Robin to whom I am referring was quite different ... Did I tell you that I think my brother Freddie may have been a Lord? But he never told me. If I'd asked him when he was in a good humour he might have said he was the Duke of something. But otherwise he'd have told me to go to hell."

The following morning I was in my bath when Willie shuffled through my bedroom and came and stood over me as I lay in the bath.

"Good-morning," I said.

"What was that?" he demanded.

"Good-morning," I repeated.

For a moment Willie was silent. He stood glowering down at me. "Do you know who that bath you're in belongs to?" he asked suddenly.

"Yes."

"To whom does it belong?"

"You, Willie."

"And who is going to use it when you've finished with it?"

"I simply don't know," I answered.

Willie shook his head and shuffled out. But over cocktails that morning, before lunch, his mood changed. "I hope we're going to have a substantial meal, Alan," he said.

"You can rely on it," Alan answered, smiling.

Then Willie turned to me. "Does my nephew Robin look like you?" he asked.

"Precisely," I replied.

"Then he must be a charming person."

"Thank you," I said.

Since he was in a good mood I thought I would get Willie to talk about his writing. "When you write a novel how do the characters occur to you?" I asked.

"Oh, I don't know," Willie said. "I used just to think of someone who attracted my interest for some reason or another and write about him. Now, can we go into lunch?"

He was pleased with the lobster mousse: "*Ça se mange assez bien*," he said. "You know, it's really quite eatable. At least I still have an appetite."

"And your royalties still flow in," I said.

"So do the fan-letters," Alan added.

"And I don't care a tinker's cuss," Willie said. "As Alan will tell you, cataracts have formed on both my eyes so I can't go through any of the letters myself and my favourite pastime—reading—is now denied to me."

"What is the happiest memory of your life?" I asked, to change the subject.

"I can't think of a single one," Willie answered.

*   *   *

On my very last visit to the Villa Mauresque, Willie was in bed. I went upstairs and sat beside him. He was asleep. He looked like a shrivelled doll, pale and very weak. Outside, the garden seemed very quiet. There was no one in sight. Only the sound of the cicadas and the song of the birds could be heard. A green light filtered through the slats of the shutters. A shaft of sunshine struck the photograph of Willie's mother on the bedside table. Willie opened his eyes. He turned his head towards

178

me and spoke as if resuming a conversation begun some while ago.

"You know, so far as I am concerned," Willie said, "life's been rather like a party that was very nice to start with but has become rather noisy as time went on. And I'm not at all sorry to go home ... I wrote that in a play once ... But I wish I *could* believe that I shall go home."

Willie's eyes flickered towards the photograph on the beside table. "I wish I could think that I would meet my darling mother—and see that wicked Gerald again ... But I certainly can't ..." He took my hand. "You don't believe that one can lose one's soul so completely in this life that there's nothing left—do you?" he asked.

I shook my head.

"The Hindus have a notion that the soul passes from one body to enter on an endless course of reincarnation," Willie continued. "They believe that what we do in our past life and what we do in our present life determines what is going to happen to us in a future life ... and this is at once an explanation and a justification of all the evil in this world ... so my soul may be reincarnated again." Willie gave a flicker of a smile. "And perhaps I'll do better next time," he said. He sighed. "I can't pray for my soul," he said. "I gave up praying when I was a small boy. And besides, I'm too far gone." Willie paused for a moment and stared up at me. "But you will pray for me, won't you?" he asked. I nodded my head. "That would be extremely kind," Willie said.

Willie's head fell back gently against the pillows. He began to doze again. I got up and walked quietly from the room, closing the door behind me. I walked slowly towards the writing-room. I moved into it and wandered slowly past the shelves, full of eighty of Willie's novels and plays—each of them with the Maugham colophon, the sign against the Evil Eye, engraved on it. I ran my hand along the line of books. Then I moved down the marble stairs, past the gilt statue of Buddha, into the dark hall. I walked towards the front door. As I opened the door, a blaze of bright sunshine from the gravel drive outside flooded the hallway. Slowly I walked out of the villa, closing the door behind me.

*　　*　　*

On Saturday evening, December 11th, after reading the news of Willie's illness in the newspaper, I telephoned to Alan at the Villa Mauresque. He was extremely distraught, but gradually he unfolded the story to me. Early on Friday morning, December 10th, Willie had had a bad fall. He had fallen again later in the day and been taken to his bedroom and put to bed. At about one a.m. on Saturday morning Alan heard him call. He ran through the communicating bathroom into the bedroom and found Willie had fallen out of bed. The effect of this third fall was to jar Willie's brain into a short period of ten minutes' lucidity, and he said to Alan: "This time I know I'm going to die, and I'm happy that I've come to for a moment because now I can say good-bye to you."

At this stage Alan burst into tears on the telephone; he was obviously in a great state of anguish. "I want you to promise me one thing," Willie had continued. "I want you to let me die in my bed."

This Alan promised to do. But later Willie had another fall, and when Alan rushed in to see him it was to discover that he was paralysed down his left side and had gone into a coma.

In the morning when the doctors came they told Alan

that if he did not allow Willie to be moved into the Anglo-American Hospital at Nice he might conceivably be accused of having killed Willie; and so, very much against his will, Alan agreed to let Willie be transported to hospital in an ambulance and accompanied him, together with a doctor.

At the time I telephoned Alan on Saturday, Willie was in a deep coma.

*   *   *

At six o'clock on the night of Sunday December 12th, I was telephoned by my cousin, and close friend, Liza—Willie's daughter, Lady Glendevon. She was very upset and had decided with her husband John to telephone me because they wanted my advice on various points.

Alan had said to her on the telephone that morning that in the event of Willie's death, Willie had left instructions that Alan—and Alan alone—should take the body to Marseilles which housed the nearest crematorium in the area.

Liza asked me whether I thought that she ought to go. And without hesitation I replied no; I felt there was no reason for her to do so.

Liza said that her house was surrounded by the press and that the telephone had been ringing all day with reporters asking her why she did not fly out. I told her she could say to the press that neither she nor I was flying out as Willie was in a coma and he had asked that his devoted companion, Alan Searle, should follow his body to the crematorium alone. After the cremation, Alan was to take the casket to England and thence to King's School, Canterbury, where it was to be buried. Alan said that Willie had insisted on having no service whatsoever.

Liza asked me my opinion as to whether I thought there should be a service or not.

"After all," Liza said, "it can't really harm him."

I replied that I agreed with her entirely and that I thought that quite apart from the fact that it would be very odd to have no service at all, I felt that the Canterbury authorities might refuse to have Willie buried in consecrated ground without a service of some kind, or at least a few prayers.

Liza said she was thankful that I had given that opinion.

Next, she asked me about the kind of funeral service I thought there should be—private or public. I replied, without hesitation, that I thought it should be private, with the family only.

Liza then said: "Thank heavens that you have given to every question the answer that John and I hoped you would give, because that's what we felt ourselves, and we feel most comforted."

Liza said she was getting in touch with the headmaster of King's School, Canterbury, the Rev. Mr Newell and with Mrs Newell. I said that I had met them and found them both most pleasant people and most understanding and sympathetic.

*   *   *

Willie died in the hospital on December 16th, but his body was driven back to the Mauresque and put in his own bed because there is some complication under French law if a person does not die in their own home. Alan was left alone with the corpse.

"We've made so many journeys together," Willie had often said to Alan, "promise me that on my last journey of all, you'll accompany me. Promise me you'll be alone when you take my body to the mortuary in Marseilles."

So Alan drove alone, following the hearse to Marseilles. Then he had to watch the coffin sliding into the furnace.

The ashes which had been placed in a casket were sent by 'plane by Alan from the south of France to England. They were taken by Willie's daughter Liza to his old school, King's School, Canterbury. It had been Willie's wish that his remains should be buried there privately in the school precincts in the shadow of the cathedral. It is interesting to note that Willie should have made lavish donations to the school which as a child he had so detested—as can be seen from many passages in *Of Human Bondage*—and should have chosen the same school as his final resting-place.

The funeral took place on a bleak December morning. Dark wintry clouds hung low over the cathedral. A procession of Willie's family went to the library which Willie had given to the school—led by the Dean. This was the only concession to ceremony.

Willie's daughter Liza and her husband were of course present, so were my sisters and myself and my nephews. Willie's ashes were in a plain mahogany casket with two red seals on it and a plate with the inscription "Somerset Maugham 1874-1965". In the centre of the lawn, beneath the walls of the library, the turf had been neatly removed and laid on one side. A small grave had been dug—a yard square. Around it were five simple wreaths. From the headmaster and the boys of King's School there was a replica in white carnations and violets of the school coat of arms which was laid alongside the little grave by the senior boy. Around the casket were wreaths from Liza and her family. The fifth spray of flowers came from "Skipper Brittle and the crew of the tanker *Somerset Maugham*."

Ranged to the left of the grave was a semi-circle of boys in their school uniforms; they varied in age from fourteen to eighteen. To the right stood the small group of mourners. Close to the grave stood the Dean who conducted the Committal Service. The Headmaster said a short prayer. The casket was lowered into the ground. Slender, leafless branches waved in the wind as the funeral procession moved slowly away.

*   *   *

Later, a plaque of stone was put into the wall of the library close to the grave. The letters K.S.C. stand for King's School, Canterbury. The engraved plaque reads:

WILLIAM SOMERSET MAUGHAM

K.S.C. 1885–1889

BORN 1874—DIED 1965